STEVE BACKLUND
with JIM BAKER

HELP!
I'M A PASTOR
PRACTICAL WISDOM FOR CHURCH LEADERS

© copyright 2014 Steve Backlund, Igniting Hope Ministries
www.IgnitingHope.com

Cover Design: Robert Schwendenmann
Interior Layout and Formatting: Robert Schwendenmann
Typesetting: Julie Heth
Cover photography: Sam Kim
Cover photograph pastor: Steve Moore
Cover photograph congregation: Steve Backlund, Megan Cotton, Laura Hardesty, Julie Heth, Levi Hug, Joellah Lutz, Ruth Moore, Julie Mustard, Adriana Pleisu, Justin Ratliff, Robert Schwendenmann, Sally Shaw, Katrina Smith.
Contributing authors: Steve Backlund, Jim Baker, Julie Heth, Steve Moore, Julie Mustard, Brendon Russell.
Editors: Melissa Amato, Julie Heth, Julie Mustard, Sophie Cotton, Heidi O'Brien, Darla Searle, Brendon Russell.
Special assistance by: Julia Graham, Joshua Keurentjes, Tara Nielsen, Marcia Russell, Sally Shaw.
Special thanks to: St. Luke's Anglican Church (Redding, California) and Tim Walls at JCI Marketing (Redding, California).

ISBN-10: 0989472531

ISBN-13: 978-0-989-47253-1

HELP!
I'M A PASTOR

DEDICATION

This book is dedicated to the senior pastors Wendy and I have served under. I am so grateful for what we have received from each of them.

FRED MUSTER
Integrity and hunger for God

WINSTON CULP
Trust and rest

JERRY CHILSON
Vision and priority of family

JERRY FROST
Love and humility

ERIC JOHNSON
Excellence and wisdom

BILL JOHNSON
Risk taking and releasing the supernatural

TABLE OF CONTENTS

TABLE OF CONTENTS

ABOUT THE AUTHORS

STEVE BACKLUND

Steve Backlund, and his wife, Wendy, are revivalist teachers, hope igniters, and itinerant ministers. Steve is an associate pastor at Bethel Church in Redding, California and teaches leadership development in both the ministry school and through Global Legacy's online school. Steve and Wendy have three children and six grandchildren. They are also the founders of Igniting Hope Ministries, emphasizing joy, hope, and higher perspectives for life and ministry. Steve has written numerous books, including *Victorious Mindsets, Let's Just Laugh at That, Igniting Faith in 40 Days,* and *Possessing Joy.* You can learn more about Steve and Wendy's ministry at their website ignitinghope.com.

JIM BAKER

"In January of 2013, I (Steve) told Jim about the vision and format for this book – with its diverse and humorous scenarios. He came alive and began sharing some outrageous happenings in his ministry, and how he approached them. I had already grown to appreciate Jim's wisdom, insight, integrity, and supernatural edge on ministry, but this conversation convinced me that our relationship needed to include doing this book together.

Jim and his wife, Mary, have three sons. Jim is passionate about seeing Heaven invade earth, evidenced by signs, wonders, miracles, and healing. He is the author of the books *The Jesus School of Healing* and *How Heaven Invades Your Finances.* He is a gift to the body of Christ, and I am blessed to introduce him to some of you for the first time." – Steve

FOREWORD

"I wish I would have been taught THAT in seminary or Bible school."

I am sure pastors think this often. I know I did. I felt unprepared for many of the challenges I faced in my seventeen years of being a senior leader of a church.

I currently have the privilege of spending much time with church leaders and future church leaders. During the last few years, I have traveled to an average of eighty different ministries a year, and I also teach a weekly class on church leadership in the Bethel School of Supernatural Ministry (BSSM) in Redding, California. My life is immersed in what is happening in the church.

One of the tools I have used in BSSM is giving the students hypothetical scenarios to discuss how they would approach particular situations. In talking through these scenarios with students, I realized how beneficial they were for developing philosophies and core values to help them with future leadership challenges. This became the impetus for writing this book.

Help! I Am a Pastor **is not just for senior pastors, but for every church leader or future church leader.** It is ideal for:

- Senior pastors
- Staff members
- Small group leaders
- Elders or board members
- Church planters
- Anyone who wants to be a strength in their ministry

This book does not attempt to be the final word on the topics covered, but it is designed to inspire you to think through your own beliefs and core values to prepare you for great days ahead in shepherding God's people.

I have appreciated working with Jim Baker on this project. His experience, insight, and creativity have added much to this writing. My team (especially Julie Heth, Steve Moore, Julie Mustard, and Brendon Russell) have also contributed significantly with their insights and practical assistance.

We bless you as you read *Help! I Am a Pastor*. It is our desire it will ignite your hope, your love, your insights, your team unity, your evangelism and church growth, and your joy. I declare you will never be the same again.

Abounding in Hope,

Steve Backlund
Igniting Hope Ministries

HOW TO USE THIS BOOK

Help! I Am a Pastor is divided up into two parts. The first section is made up of life and leadership core values for leaders. The second section includes fifty common church scenarios.

LIFE AND LEADERSHIP CORE VALUES

I have included eighty of my guiding principles for leadership and ministry. These have come from my own experience, my constant interaction with other leaders, and my association with the leaders at Bethel Church in Redding, California. This is not intended to be an exhaustive list, but it does address most of the things we will face in ministry.

I urge you to meditate on these core values. Ask the Holy Spirit to help you know which are to be emphasized now and which are for a later season. These eighty fundamental beliefs will help you become more intentional in your life and ministry. Also, as you share these in your leadership team, it will help create greater unity and clarity in responding to situations that arise in church life.

THE SCENARIOS

These are presented on two pages and include the following:

THE SCENARIO

This describes an event which is common in church life. I have injected humor into these through people's names and in the story itself. As you smile or laugh, you will most likely say, "Yes, I have experienced something like this before."

LIES ASSOCIATED WITH THIS SCENARIO

Jesus said, "The truth will make you free," and Romans 12:2 says, "Be transformed by the renewing of your mind." Our beliefs will ultimately have the greatest impact on what we experience. This section will help you identify common lies connected to the scenario that often restrict breakthrough. One spiritual weapon to help overcome these lies is laughter. Lies sound very real when they are just in our thoughts, but they sound laughable when we speak them out of our mouths. When you read these lies in the book, we suggest you take time to actually laugh out loud concerning them.

LIFE AND LEADERSHIP CORE VALUES TO CONSIDER

I take five of the eighty core values and apply them to the scenario. By doing so, I am guiding you to respond with God's established wisdom in your life, rather than reacting to challenges emotionally or impulsively.

HOW TO USE THIS BOOK

DISCERNING WHAT GOD IS DEVELOPING IN ME

We are all being prepared for greater influence in the days ahead, and each situation we face creates an opportunity for us to get stronger in our life and leadership. The more vision we have for the future, the more purpose and power we have for the present. This section helps you focus on what is being developed in you as you determine your course of action.

QUESTIONS TO ASK BEFORE TAKING ACTION

No two situations are the same even if they are about the same issue. These questions will help you determine how large the problem is and help you see the bigger picture of what is happening.

PRACTICAL STEPS TO CONSIDER

I give you three ideas of how to approach the situation. These steps themselves are full of good overall insight for church leadership, but they also are a practical demonstration of how to apply the core values into leading a ministry. I am not saying these are the only actions to take, but I believe you will find them very helpful.

DECLARATIONS

Jesus did not think his way out of the wilderness in Matthew 4, but he spoke his way out. One of the greatest tools for mind renewal is having the habit of making declarations. If we are going to believe something different, then we need to hear something different (Romans 10:17). I encourage you to say these declarations aloud to accelerate the transformation in your life.

LIFE AND LEADERSHIP CORE VALUES

1. **There is always a solution for every situation I face** – This is one of the most important core values to have as a leader. It could be used in every scenario in this book, but we will remind you of it in situations which really need a hope upgrade. "Leaders are brokers of hope" (Napoleon Bonaparte). Somebody has to hope if transformation, change, and breakthrough are to occur. This truth is a hope anchor.
   Supporting verses: 1 Corinthians 10:13, Luke 1:37, Matthew 17:20

2. **I strongly prioritize and protect my "secret place" times with the Lord** – In Acts 6 the Apostles set the example by selecting deacons so they could give themselves "continually to prayer and the ministry of the word" (Acts 6:4). Jesus also withdrew Himself for times alone with His Father. I follow this emphasis for my own life. Even in seasons of busyness, I have creative strategies to keep my heart connection with God strong.
   Supporting verses: Acts 6:1-4, Luke 5:16

3. **I build "bridges" in my teachings to help people move into the deeper things of God** – I honor people's need to understand the scriptural support for what I am saying, as well as my personal testimony concerning the emphasis I am making. When I share truths that challenge old paradigms, I strategically say something like, "This is what I am not saying...," to help people mentally grasp what I am saying.
   Supporting verses: Acts 17:11, 1 Corinthians 9:20

4. **I lead a ministry that inspires individuals to love the Bible and read it consistently** – It is obvious how important the Bible is to our ministry and to me. We create a contagious love for the Bible in our ministry.
   Supporting verses: 1 Peter 2:2, Acts 17:11

5. **I equip people with the basic principles of how to interpret the Bible** – I realize one of the most important things I do as a pastor is to help people personally connect with God. One aspect of this is to give them tools to know how to interpret scripture.
   Supporting verses: Hebrews 4:12, 2 Timothy 3:16-17

6. **I lead a culture of radical encouragement** – I lead in encouraging others. I do so by giving specific thanks to people regularly. Our leadership spends time encouraging and prophesying over each other. I even find ways to encourage people with "issues" because I know everyone's negative qualities are positive qualities out of whack.
   Supporting verses: Hebrews 10:24-25, Isaiah 35:4-7

LIFE AND LEADERSHIP CORE VALUES

7. **My team and I pursue spiritual fathers and mothers we mutually respect** – It is a great safeguard to have leaders from the outside who can give input to help in times of difficulty, to bring wisdom in decisions being made, and to provide healthy accountability for the leadership team. I intentionally pursue these relationships. I "date" guest speakers relationally to see which of them could fulfill this fathering or mothering role. Once it is clear that someone is to serve in this role, I strategically invite him or her to come to our ministry on a regular basis, and I find other ways to connect with them.
Supporting verses: 1 Corinthians 4:15, 2 Kings 2:6

8. **I pursue "buy-in" from leaders and key people involved before making a big decision** – In every situation possible, I have important people involved in the decision-making process (instead of me just telling them what the decisions are). I realize when someone "buys in" to where I am leading (feeling part of the decision-making process and concluding with me on the course of action to be taken), it increases the likelihood of success and decreases the likelihood of relational problems in the future.
Supporting verses: Acts 11:1-18, Acts 13:1-3

9. **I build a culture of feedback in my ministry that I lead by example** – a) I set the tone for personal growth in the ministry by being passionate for personal improvement. b) I am open about areas I desire to grow more in. c) I create healthy systems where I receive feedback from those I lead about how I am leading. d) I create space for feedback in ministries and leadership relationships (I commonly use the phrase, "Please share with me two things you appreciate about how I led that meeting and one thing I can improve on").
Supporting verses: Proverbs 15:22, Proverbs 19:20

10. **I create opportunities for those in my church to encounter God in powerful ways** – I proactively plan happenings in our schedule which increase the likelihood that people will encounter God in significant ways. I personally stay hungry for these fresh encounters. I believe one encounter with God can often do more than years of teaching and counseling.
Supporting verses: Acts 1:4, Acts 4:31

11. **I recognize the tendency that current moves of God are often persecuted by those impacted by a previous move of God** – Because of this, I withhold judgment against new things happening (or new doctrinal emphasis) until I actually understand what is happening. I realize most great truths or outpourings are "messy" at first. I will not let excesses or weird spiritual happenings cause me to do a pendulum swing reaction to the other extreme. I will always look for what God is doing in the midst of seeming excesses or apparent theological extremes.
Supporting verses: Matthew 23:1-12, Acts 4:18-22

12. **I go the extra mile in honesty and in establishing accountability concerning how ministry money is handled** – I understand carelessness about ministry finances is a character issue that will hinder the trust others have for me. I reject the deceptive feeling of entitlement based on how much I sacrifice for the ministry. I know it is better to "lose" in the short term by being extra honest and accountable, because I will win in the long term by having such integrity. *Supporting verses: Titus 2:7-8, Proverbs 28:18*

13. **I refuse to blame those I lead for the quality of our ministry** – Once I believe I am a victim of the people I lead, I stop leading (the people's behaviors and attitudes now lead me). Therefore, I do not ignore problems, but I am careful not to label my people in a negative way based on their behavior. *Supporting verse: Ephesians 4:11-16*

14. **I am more concerned about building people than I am concerned about building a ministry** – I purpose to create an environment where people can thrive in life, ministry, family, and in the dreams they have in their hearts. I do not see those in my ministry as servants or slaves of my vision or the mission of the church. I certainly call people to a deep commitment to these things, but I stay focused on the fact that our ministry is a "launching pad" for people to grow in their gifts and influence society in incredible ways. *Supporting verses: 2 Timothy 2:2, Ephesians 4:11-16*

15. **I consistently follow through on what I say I will do** – I am a person of commitment. I follow through on the big and small things I say I will do. If I find myself flippantly saying I will do things without really planning to, I will develop a plan for greater follow-through, or I will stop committing to things I am not planning to do. *Supporting verses: James 5:12, Matthew 5:37*

16. **I embrace seasons of building trust in the eyes of those I lead** – In any ministry assignment I have, one of my first priorities is to behave in a trustworthy manner. I realize if people do not trust me as their leader, I will need to manipulate and use fear to control them in order for them to follow my leadership. *Supporting verses: 1 Peter 3:1, Acts 27:10,11,21-44*

17. **I thrive in uncertainty, difficulty, and unresolved situations because I have a "word" from the Lord** – The quality of my life depends on my identifying what God has spoken to me. I can thrive in the appearance of outward non-success if I know what God has promised and what He has directed me to do. I realize the foundation of my leadership is rooted in identifying what God has spoken to me. *Supporting verses: Matthew 4:4, 1 Timothy 1:18, Ephesians 6:17*

18. **In any people group my ministry wants to influence, I look for the "son of peace" (or "daughter of peace") to work through** – Jesus told his disciples to do this in Luke 10:5. When they went to a new city, they were to find a person to primarily work through in order to reach the people there. I embrace this profound strategy in reaching people, whether in another nation or in a group in our area such as youth, seniors, young adults, business people, or others.
Supporting verses: Luke 10:5, 2 Timothy 2:2

19. **I have a supernatural personal story as the basis for seemingly risky and illogical things I do** – I understand faith is often spelled R.I.S.K., and this risk-taking is propelled by clear, divinely inspired events. The Bible is full of people who took illogical actions based on a story they had from God (e.g. Peter in Acts 10, Joseph in Matthew 1:20-25, Moses in Exodus 3, and Saul in 1 Samuel 9). I, and the ministry I lead, have personal and corporate "God stories" we repeat often concerning His direction and purpose for us.
Supporting verses: Matthew 1:20-25, Acts 11:1-18

20. **I proactively anticipate challenges that could occur in the future** – I have an unusual ability to see and prepare for what is coming. I am like a sports coach who has scouted the opposition in order to tell his team what to expect. This is not a spirit of foreboding or a Numbers 13 "ten spy syndrome," but this wisdom gift helps the ministry avoid many problems by preventing them or dealing with them when they are small. "The prudent sees the evil and hides himself."
Supporting verses: Proverbs 22:3, Proverbs 27:12

21. **When people are struggling in life, I first seek to increase their connection to the Lord** – Before I utilize counseling techniques, I realize many people's problems will disappear if they connect or reconnect spiritually with God. The fruit of the Spirit in Galatians 5:22-23 comes from a healthy union with God, not by human effort; therefore, I often prescribe "mega doses" of God's Word and His Spirit to those needing help. These prescriptions are "homework" assignments and include getting into consistent fellowship, Bible intake, audio messages, praying with a prayer partner, and attending special meetings.
Supporting verses: Matthew 6:33, Haggai 1

22. **I pursue relationships with the strong influencers in places I am called to lead** – I want to know the heart of the people influencing our ministry, whether they are official leaders or strong personalities without a ministry title. I also want them to get to know my heart. I realize it is not wisdom to empower people to influence our ministry when there is not a good heart connection between them and the church leadership team.
Supporting verses: Acts 17:16-17, Acts 18:24-18

23. **I live and demonstrate the gospel supernaturally** – I purpose to live a life and lead a ministry where the power of God is demonstrated. I will not be satisfied simply with good programs and well-crafted messages, but I will lead the way to see the Book of Acts become a growing reality in our midst.
Supporting verses: 1 Corinthians 2:1-4, Mark 16:17-18

24. **My leaders and I frequently ask the question, "What is the Holy Spirit saying to us?"** – I believe this question keeps us from depending on principles, and it helps us be open for the "now word" ("Rhema" word) for us. I realize many great breakthroughs began because someone heard the "proceeding word of the Lord." Our ministry is growing in walking in the "Sons of Issachar anointing" which "understands times and seasons" and knows what we are to do.
Supporting verses: Matthew 4:4, 1 Chronicles 12:32

25. **I believe people's negative qualities are usually immature characteristics of positive qualities in their life** – I identify the positive side of the negative traits I see in people's lives. As much as possible, I affirm the good part of their tendencies. As I do this, it increases my heart connection with them, and it increases the likelihood I can help bring any needed adjustments in their lives.
Supporting verses: Matthew 26:35, Genesis 37:11

26. **I err on the side of allowing too much Holy Spirit activity, rather than too little** – I understand that if a primary goal of my leadership is to prevent "wild fire," then we will probably not have the real fire of God in our midst. I do not have an "anything goes" philosophy, but I am not quick to conclude new or unusual spiritual phenomenon is not of God. Scripture does say "all things must be done decent and in order," but I remind myself that cemeteries are some of the most decent and in order places in existence (and there is not much life there).
Supporting verse: 1 Corinthians 14:26

27. **I process unverified information about others in a healthy way** – I do not passively listen to hearsay about others. I keep my beliefs strong about those who are being talked about. I trust God to help me not be gullible, but I do not allow gossip or random comments to shape my beliefs about others.
Supporting verses: 1 Timothy 5:19, Proverbs 18:17

28. **I regularly educate our people about our ministry's philosophy and process of decision making** – I do this especially with matters that could be controversial or confusing. As much as possible, I share the behind-the-scenes processes for decision making and the development of ministry philosophies for crucial areas of church life. I have a great ability to communicate this in sermons and in other settings. This sharing helps people see the bigger picture for what is happening.
Supporting verses: 1 Corinthians 14, Acts 6:2-6

29. **I purposely do not overly plan meetings, so there will be an increased likelihood of a "suddenly" of God happening** – I realize being constantly rushed to get things done in meetings limits what the Holy Spirit could do in the way of miracles, prophecy, and in other ways. Even though we have different kinds of meetings (with some being designed for more spontaneous Holy Spirit outbreaks), I intentionally leave room for a "suddenly" to happen. Note: It is also good to regularly end on time when you have stated an ending time for a board meeting or other meeting.
    Supporting verses: 1 Thessalonians 5:19, Luke 24:49

30. **I tell those I lead who they are much more than I tell them what to do** – I understand it is very difficult for people to do what they do not believe they are; therefore, I spend more time telling them who they are in Christ than I do telling them what to do as Christians. Just as the angel unlocked Gideon's future by telling him who he really was (even though he was not yet experiencing that), I do the same for my people.
    Supporting verses: Romans 4:17-19, Judges 6:12

31. **Those who have influence within our ministry are known and trusted** – Because we desire to create a safe place for those who come to our ministry, we prioritize relationships with people in our ministry who are known to have a lifestyle that is loving, powerful, and positive in its influence. We give time for "body ministry" (people encouraging, helping, or praying for one another) and are open to God bringing someone not known by us to impact us, but that is not the norm.
    Supporting verses: Acts 6:3, 1 Timothy 3:2-7

32. **I "date" people in key ministry relationships before "marrying" them with a title** – I do not let initial feelings of excitement for someone lead me to "marry" them into an important ministry position. I, and my team, take time to understand if this potential leader is ready for the level of responsibility we would give him or her and to see if we are compatible in working together. I create opportunities for people to participate and contribute to our ministry in order to "test" the strength of our relationship and the person's readiness for a greater ministry.
    Supporting verses: 1 Timothy 3:10, Acts 6:3

33. **I measure success by how many of our people are advancing the kingdom outside of the church walls** – I do not measure my success by how many people come to church on a Sunday. I raise up disciples, not just church attenders. I am not paid by the church to do the work of the ministry, but I am paid to equip the saints for the work of the ministry. We purpose to increase in numbers, but our main focus is to send our people into every realm of society (government, education, business, arts, media, and more).
    Supporting verses: Ephesians 4:11-12, Luke 10:1-9

LIFE AND LEADERSHIP CORE VALUES

34. **I seek to understand who I am to people and the role I have in their lives** – I do not assume that people see me as a prime influencer in their life. I determine my place in people's lives through discernment and asking good questions.
Supporting verses: 1 Corinthians 9:20, James 1:5

35. **I adapt my leadership and relational emphasis according to the culture I am in** – Just as missionaries to foreign countries adapt their lifestyle and emphasis according to the culture they are sent to, I do the same for the people I am called to. I reject the temptation to force my brand of Christianity on them. I trust God for wisdom in how to relate to them, love them, and reach them without compromising the gospel or my godly principles.
Supporting verses: 1 Corinthians 9:20, Acts 17:22-33

36. **We comply with all legal requirements set by the government, yet do not compromise our biblical beliefs and integrity** – We do not run a careless and disorganized ministry but one that is filled with excellence and integrity. We also have an up to date constitution and bylaws to help guide our ministry.
Supporting verses: Romans 13:1-7, 1 Peter 2:17

37. **My faithfulness in small things opens doors for bigger opportunities** – I believe there is no shortcut to living a life of continual increase. If we bypass the development of our character, our integrity, and our following through on our commitments, we will not be able to lead people; it will not matter how anointed we are. Those who do small things in a great way will tap into a spiritual principle that will bring greater things into our lives.
Supporting verses: Matthew 25:23, Luke 16:10

38. **I pastor a city and region, not just a local church** – I have taken ownership in my spirit for the people of my area. I purpose to be a positive influence to every person, ministry, and institution in my area.
Supporting verses: Acts 1:8, Matthew 28:18-20

39. **I am more focused on my personal growth than in bringing change to those I am called to influence** – My continued growth as a person and leader is the number one thing I do to influence my culture and the people I am surrounded by. I do not have a ministry because I have a message – I have a ministry because I have a life others want to follow.
Supporting verses: Matthew 7:5, 1 Timothy 4:16

40. **I live with intentionality by having a clear set of priorities, which dictate how I spend my time** – I am proactive, not reactive. I fill my calendar up with the important things of life, so I do not live a life of simply reacting to the urgent demands around me. I deliberately place the following in my calendar: time with God, time with family, personal growth activities, meetings with leaders and potential leaders, days off, and team meetings.
Supporting verses: Matthew 6:33, Acts 6:2-4

41. **I decrease gossip in our ministry by setting the example of speaking directly with the people that I have a problem with and inviting them to speak directly with me** – I have a plan to reduce the reasons gossip and grumbling exist in a ministry. Common reasons include: a) It is thought to be normal. b) Leadership has created few or no avenues for people to ask questions or share concerns. c) Leadership does not create a culture of helping their people "buy-in" to directions taken. d) There is not a sufficient focus on people receiving emotional healing. e) Leadership does not equip their people with the tools to deal successfully with the root issues behind gossip or with the proper biblical steps to take when they have a problem with a person.
Supporting verses: Matthew 18:15-17, Proverbs 27:17

42. **I am primarily a developer of leaders** – One of my main focuses is to train others to lead and to shepherd people. I increasingly spend my time with leaders and potential leaders, rather than on fixing the problems of everyone within our ministry. Whenever possible, I employ the following process to raise up leaders for specific areas: a) have someone assist me (or assist one of my key leaders) and watch how I/we lead, b) co-lead with this person, c) "assist" them as they lead, d) have them lead without me/us with a good plan established for continued leadership growth, accountability, and encouragement.
Supporting verses: Ephesians 4:11-12, 2 Timothy 2:2

43. **I am honoring in attitudes and words I have about those in authority over me (even when I disagree with them)** – I realize that how I respond to imperfect leaders over me is one indicator of how ready I am to lead at a higher level.
Supporting verses: 1 Samuel 24:1-11, Ephesians 6:1-3

44. **I seek to listen and understand before I seek to be heard and understood** – I am committed to understanding the people in my life. I am a great question asker. I make sure I can communicate effectively the feelings of those I am talking with before I share my feelings.
Supporting verses: James 1:19-20, Proverbs 18:13

45. **I give generously in the areas where I have need** – Luke 6:37-38 teaches us the principle of giving in the specific area of our need. "Judge not, and you shall not be judged. Condemn not, and you shall not be condemned. Forgive, and you will be forgiven. Give, and it will be given to you... For with the same measure that you use, it will be measured back to you." We are told if we "give" forgiveness, we receive "forgiveness," and if we "judge not," we will not be judged. Therefore, whether I need finances, leaders, a new building, a healthy marriage, or increased manifest power in ministry, I see giving into the area of need as part of the strategy to see breakthrough.
Supporting verses: Luke 8:37-28, Galatians 6:7-8

LIFE AND LEADERSHIP
CORE VALUES

46. **The anointing brings great breakthrough, but it is hearing and believing truth that makes us free** – I am hungry to be in environments with a great anointing, but I am more hungry to believe truth because this is ultimately what will make me free.
Supporting verses: John 8:31, 32, Romans 12:2

47. **I equip those I lead to be financially successful so they can be trusted with true spiritual riches** – Our ministry trains people to be successful in every area o f life, including finances. I believe the Parable of the Talents in Matthew 25 implies every person is endowed with the ability to increase, and Luke 16:11 reveals healthy financial stewardship is the "kindergarten" of being able to receive true spiritual riches. Our church offers necessary training to help people budget, get out of debt, learn how to give consistently, build wealth, and succeed in business and the workplace.
Supporting verses: Luke 16:11, Deuteronomy 8:18

48. **My response to something is almost always more important than the something** – I live a life and lead a ministry where we inspire people to thrive on the inside when there is difficulty on the outside. This does not mean we are passive or do not ever confront wrong, but we understand it is generally unwise to emotionally respond to negative happenings.
Supporting verses: James 1:2-4, Romans 5:3-4, 3 John 2

49. **I am "sent" by trustworthy people into the ministry I have, and I continue to pursue personal accountability with them** – It is important for my life and ministry that I have people of integrity around me. These individuals can recommend my ministry as proven, beneficial, and of good doctrine. They also can testify that my life and my ministry to my family is an example the church can follow. I have healthy accountability with these trustworthy people. This reality helps relieve anxiety that would come from being unaccountable in my life and ministry.
Supporting verses: Acts 13:1-3, 2 Timothy 2:2, 1 Timothy 3:1-11

50. **I believe people want to do the right thing; therefore, my default belief is to give the benefit of the doubt to others** – I see those I lead as saints, not sinners. Their tendency is to do right, not wrong. This affects my expectations and the language I use in talking to them. I am not trying to prevent bad from coming out of them; I am seeking to release the good that is in them. This does not mean I am naive about their past or current situations, but I choose to see them as God does – knowing that one of the most powerful things I can do as a leader is to believe in those I lead.
Supporting verses: 1 Corinthians 13:7, 2 Corinthians 5:17, Colossians 1:21-22

51. **I focus more on heart connections than outward obedience toward those I lead** – The quality of our ministry ultimately is dependent on the quality of relationships we have within the ministry – especially among the leadership team. Because of this, I prioritize heart connections with those I lead. This is more important to me than their obedience to me. Additionally, I emphasize to all my leaders the priority of heart connections in the groups they lead.
Supporting verses: Colossians 3:21, 4:1, Ephesians 6:4

52. **I am a God-pleaser, not a people-pleaser** – I have dealt with the unhealthy need to have the approval of man. I am not trying to be a popular leader. I live my life in such a way that I am respected, even by those who disagree with my beliefs, decisions, and leadership. I am willing to make unpopular decisions based on integrity, purity, biblical truths, and on what I believe God has said.
Supporting verses: Galatians 1:10, Proverbs 29:25

53. **I help people understand how their behavior impacts others** – I do this by creating a culture of regular feedback. I invite people to help me understand how my behavior affects them and others. I create structures within my leadership team that help them do the same. I am unafraid to give constructive criticism to others about behaviors that are hurtful or that are reducing their favor in the eyes of others.
Supporting verses: Proverbs 12:1, 1 Corinthians 14:23

54. **I have high standards in how I conduct myself in relationships with the opposite sex** – I avoid the appearance of evil. I refrain from any type of flirting, suggestive comments, or talking about emotional or sexual needs with anyone who could be tempted to become emotionally or intimately involved with me. I proactively discuss our high standards in this area with my leadership team.
Supporting verses: 1 Thessalonians 5:22, Colossians 3:5

55. **I have an abundance mentality instead of a lack mentality** – I believe there is more than enough to thrive and walk in blessing in every situation I am in. My expectation of God's goodness drives out fear.
Supporting verses: Ephesians 3:20, Philippians 4:19

56. **I avoid the appearance of evil in all I do** – I realize as a leader I am held to a higher standard in what I do in my life. I not only teach with words but more importantly by my actions, including what I do and what I do not do. I therefore restrict myself to not participate in behaviors that would cause weaker Christians to stumble. I obviously am not going to be controlled by religious legalists, but I gladly embrace limiting certain things I do as an act of love and maturity in my leadership.
Supporting verses: Romans 14:13, 1 Timothy 4:12

57. **I purpose to have my family respect me more than the people I lead respect me** – My real ministry starts when I walk through the doors of my home. If my family thinks I am genuine, then I will not have a problem with others thinking so. My ministry to my spouse and family is more important than my ministry in the church. My calendar and finances reflect this commitment.
Supporting verses: 1 Timothy 3:4-5, Titus 1:6

58. **I confront people with love and inspire them to grow by reminding them of their destiny** – A culture of honor and empowerment does not mean I do not confront, but it affects how I confront. I am not trying to make people act like "good Christians," but I do share growth opportunities from a heart of deep love and compassion. I also help people understand they cannot take certain things "with them" (including negative attitudes, lack of faithfulness, and hurtful actions) as they move toward their prophetic destiny.
Supporting verses: Galatians 6:1, Matthew 18:15-17

59. **I have a healthy process in decision making** – This includes: a) basing it on Scripture, b) having a "story from God" about the direction to pursue, c) having key people involved in the decision-making process, d) making the decision in faith, e) not changing my mind simply because of negative feelings or negative circumstances.
Supporting verses: James 1:5-8, Proverbs 15:22

60. **God works all things together for good in my ministry** – One of my strongest core values is the belief that God supernaturally works everything for my good. I do not believe everything that happens in my life is from God, but I believe even the worst of circumstances can and will be turned to good in time.
Supporting verses: Romans 8:28, Genesis 50:20

61. **I have high-level beliefs about the people I lead and desire to influence** – I believe people tend to rise to the level of the beliefs of the influencers in their lives. I keep my beliefs high about people even when their behavior requires me to have boundaries and confrontation in relationships.
Supporting verses: 1 Corinthians 13:7, Judges 6:12

62. **I understand the "times and seasons" of my ministry and what I am supposed to emphasize** – I adjust my ministry emphasis according to the season I, and the ministry, are in. I can adapt my leadership style to become more fathering, prophetic, administrative, confronting, equipping, leadership developing, empowering, or something else. I also know when it is time for another person to come into the senior leadership role, and I make way for healthy transitions in leadership.
Supporting verses: 1 Chronicles 12:32, Ecclesiastes 3:1-8

63. **Freedom does not mean that anything can happen** – I understand that having standards for who will minister in the church is not necessarily being overly controlling. I also understand that it is okay to limit some forms of expression. I help those in my ministry to understand this philosophy as well.
Supporting verses: Galatians 5:13, 1 Corinthians 14:23

64. **I am careful in the words I use regarding those I am having difficulty with** – I only talk with those who are able and committed to finding a solution. I do not make negative or random comments about people or ministries because these remarks lower my trust level in the eyes of those who hear me speaking carelessly about others.
Supporting verses: Ephesians 4:29, Proverbs 21:23

65. **I recognize that trust for one another in our leadership team is a necessary ingredient for our ministry to go forward** – Trust is the currency of long-term influence. A lack of trust for one another is a common dysfunction on ministry teams. I am keenly aware when trust for one another is decreasing, and I am quick to seek remedies when I notice lowering levels of trust.
Supporting verses: Acts 6:3, Exodus 18:21-23

66. **I motivate people through vision instead of guilt and manipulation** – I believe people want to do the right thing, and this belief is reflected in the language I use when I am trying to influence their behavior. I, and the leaders of our ministry, stay away from any form of guilt or shaming to trying to get people to do the things we believe they should do.
Supporting verses: Ephesians 6:3, 2 Corinthians 9:6-12

67. **The people of our ministry have clear, healthy avenues to share concerns they have about the church or me** – I do not give the impression that disagreeing with our leaders or me is wrong or dishonoring. Our ministry's goal is to have every regular attendee connected with at least one of our leaders. This connection is important for many reasons, including giving the people of the church someone to talk with if they do not understand or have concerns about directions being taken. Obviously, we are not going to create a culture of constant questioning of what is happening, but we do not want to go to the opposite extreme of shaming those who disagree.
Supporting verses: Matthew 18:15-17, Colossians 3:16

68. **I have a strong ability to make people feel needed, valued, and loved in our ministry as opposed to them feeling used** – I truly appreciate the people God has given me in the ministry I lead. I am able to convey this heart in public ministry and in personal interactions. I intentionally find ways to connect my heart with theirs. I take advantage of brief times of connection that present themselves to me so that my relationships with people will be stronger.
Supporting verses: 1 Corinthians 13:4-8, John 21:7

69. **Children do not have a junior Holy Spirit** – I find ways for children to feel important in our ministry. I have a multi generational mindset, and I pass revival on to the next generation. I find ways to regularly send the message that children's ministry is a great calling. We honor our children's workers at a high level.
Supporting verses: Matthew 18:5, 1 Samuel 3

70. **I am more for things than I am against things** – My life and ministry are not in reaction to the perceived wrongs of others. I am not afraid to speak the truth, but I am not critical in public, from the pulpit, or in my personal life about people, other ministries, politicians, or other entities. I am proactively moving toward God's vision and goal for me, not reactively running from problems and the wrongs I see in others.
Supporting verses: Romans 13:14, Philippians 3:12-14

71. **I take the "log" out of my own eye before trying to take the speck out of someone else's** – Whenever I am tempted to criticize, judge, or put a negative label on another person or ministry, I refocus my energies and thoughts toward improving something in my own life or ministry that relates to the area I have become judgmental about.
Supporting verses: Matthew 7:1-5, Luke 6:36-38

72. **I interview the spouse of my potential key leaders** – I want to know the heart of the spouse, and I want him or her to understand the position potentially being offered.
Supporting verses: 1 Timothy 3:11, Proverbs 24:3

73. **I intentionally associate with people who are stronger than me in key areas of life and ministry so I will become stronger in those areas** – I believe if I "hang out" with eagles, I will become an eagle (the same is true of prairie chickens). I associate with "eagles" through books I read, the conferences I attend, the classes I take, and the people I invite into my life and ministry. I intentionally connect with the people in my church who have great gifts I can tap into.
Supporting verses: Proverbs 13:20, Acts 4:13

74. **I have at least one person in my life with whom I share the deep things of my life with (things such as disappointments, weaknesses, dreams, fears, and longings)** – Every person has at least one area in their life which cannot be overcome without the help of another person. I believe this need for others creates a necessary humility in my life that helps me stay strong and avoid careless mistakes that will derail my life and ministry.
Supporting verses: James 5:16, 1 John 1:7

75. **I prioritize my emotional well-being** – I do not wait until I am falling apart to get help for myself. I pursue connection with people and ministries who have an anointing to help leaders stay healthy. It is not a sign of weakness to receive such ministry, but it is an act of love for my family and those I minister to.
Supporting verses: James 5:14-16, Isaiah 61:1

76. **I purpose to communicate sensitive matters with people face to face and not through text or email** – I understand how hearts can be misjudged through texts or emails but are more easily understood in face to face conversations. If I need to send an email about a delicate matter, I always have someone else read the email before I send it.
Supporting verses: Proverbs 15:2, Proverbs 15:22

77. **My ministry provides regular training and education on key life skills** – I understand these areas need special emphasis because they are at the root of many church and family problems. These areas include parenting, marriage, finances, time management, moral purity, communication skills, and conflict resolution. We have people in our ministry who are "specialists" in each of these areas. I also have an unusual ability to include regular wisdom on these matters in my sermons and teachings. Our ministry inspires people to value growth in these areas as a vital key to longevity and influence.
Supporting verses: Ephesians 4:11-16, 2 Timothy 2:2

78. **There is a designated person or persons who help the people of our church know how to treat a pastor** – I realize people need to be taught how to steward well the relationships they have with the senior pastors and other staff. For this reason, we identify a respected person who can be a resource to the people and say things that would be uncomfortable for the pastor to say.
Supporting verses: 1 Timothy 5:17-19, Galatians 6:6

79. **I realize the same environment that exposed a Judas also created eleven world changers** – If my goal in ministry is to prevent a Judas, I probably will not have any world changers. I will not allow disappointment or even betrayal to diminish my belief in those I lead. I expect those in my ministry to change the world.
Supporting verses: John 6:67-71, Matthew 13:24-30

80. **I regularly share testimonies of God's goodness and power as a strategy to bring our ministry into its fullness** – Faith comes by hearing, so we proactively share testimonies of the goodness of God that have manifested in healing, provision, restoration, breakthrough, and miracles in our lives and in the lives of others.
Supporting verses: Revelation 19:10, Romans 10:17

50 COMMON CHURCH SCENARIOS

MY PEOPLE ARE ALWAYS LATE FOR MEETINGS

SCENARIO

Ernie Efficient becomes the pastor at Set Free Church. On his first Sunday, he notices only a few people in the sanctuary for the 10:00 AM service. He asks the worship leader, Gordon Glory, "Where is everyone?" Gordon says, "Oh, we go by Set Free Church time here. They will be here shortly." Some minutes pass and the service starts at 10:22 AM, with the church filling up by 10:30 AM. Pastor Efficient also notices that people are regularly late for other meetings as well. He wonders whether or not he should seek to address this tardiness tendency in the church. What would you do?

LIES ASSOCIATED WITH THIS SCENARIO

- I need to be frustrated with my people until they start being on time.
- My people cannot change.
- If my people really valued God and me, they would be on time.
- Being on time is really not that important.

LIFE AND LEADERSHIP CORE VALUES TO CONSIDER

1 There is always a solution for every situation I face.
8 I pursue buy-in from leaders and key people involved before making a big decision.
51 I focus more on heart connections than outward obedience toward those I lead.
62 I understand the "times and seasons" of my ministry and what I am supposed to emphasize.
61 I have high level beliefs about the people I lead and desire to influence.

DISCERNING WHAT GOD IS DEVELOPING IN ME

- I am learning how to inspire people through vision, rather than through law.
- I have the opportunity to help my people show value to one another by valuing their time.
- I get to move my ministry into a greater degree of excellence.

QUESTIONS TO ASK BEFORE TAKING ACTION

1. What are other ministries doing to increase punctuality?
2. How important is this right now?
3. Are there any positives in people feeling free to come late?
4. Am I reacting out of frustration, or am I moving forward because of vision?

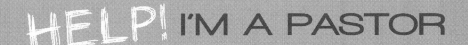
PRACTICAL STEPS TO CONSIDER

1. **Purpose to be early, not on time** – Consider communicating with the congregation that if the goal is only to be on time, then there will be no room for unexpected happenings which might cause us to be late. Those who plan to be early will give themselves room for things like heavy traffic or trying to find a misplaced item before leaving. If we are going to be early, we will need to find ways to end prior meetings on time or early, so we will not be rushed for the new one.

2. **Develop meetings before the meeting** – This is one of the best ways to increase punctuality for church meetings. It is also a wise use of time as it allows us to multiply what is happening during a particular day or evening by adding a prayer meeting, short leadership meeting, mini-training session, or coffee and fellowship time. It might be necessary to move the time of the main meeting back 30 minutes if people's schedules make it difficult to come at the time you originally set.

3. **Play a five minute countdown video before your services** – Many ministries play a five minute countdown video before their services begin. The people see the seconds running off before the start time and are encouraged to get to their seats. Many of these videos are fun and inspiring, plus countdowns create an excitement for what will happen. Lastly, the Holy Spirit is full of good ideas about increasing punctuality if we ask Him. "We have not because we ask not" (James 4:3).

DECLARATIONS

- I lead a church of increasing excellence.
- I inspire people to want to be faithful in little things, including being on time.
- I am excited about everyone who is part of my ministry, including those who consistently come late.

2 "PASTOR, THERE ARE MANY OTHERS WHO FEEL THE WAY I DO"

SCENARIO

Vij Illantee has a forceful personality and is usually not happy with how Pastor Sam Sincere is leading Let's All Get Along Church. He regularly shares with Sam his laundry list of complaints – everything from "The music is way too loud" to "You are not feeding the sheep with your messages." When he is trying to make a point of how bad things are, he says, "Pastor, there are many people in the congregation who are unhappy with your leadership, but they won't tell you. They are afraid they will hurt your feelings or that you will become angry with them. I hear this all the time from a great number of people." If you were Pastor Sam, what would you do?

LIES ASSOCIATED WITH THIS SCENARIO

*   I should not be a pastor if anyone I am leading is unhappy with my leadership.
*   If I believe I have any areas I need to improve, that would demonstrate unnecessary weakness to those I lead.
*   I should not confront Mr. Illantee on anything because he might get mad.
*   There is no doubt Vij is a messenger of Satan, and he should be asked to leave the church.

LIFE AND LEADERSHIP CORE VALUES TO CONSIDER

48 My response to something is almost always more important than the something.
58 I confront people with love and inspire them to grow by reminding them of their destiny.
67 The people of our ministry have clear, healthy avenues to share concerns they have about the church or me.
77 My ministry provides regular training and education on key life skills.
78 There is a designated person or persons who help the people of our church know how to treat a pastor.

DISCERNING WHAT GOD IS DEVELOPING IN ME

*   I am learning to deal with dysfunctional behaviors in my ministry.
*   I have the opportunity to evaluate how open I am to receiving feedback from those I lead.
*   I get to get free from an unhealthy need for people's approval.

4

HELP! I'M A PASTOR

QUESTIONS TO ASK BEFORE TAKING ACTION

1. How well do I know how the people in my ministry are feeling about my leadership?
2. What insecurities might this be stirring up in me?
3. How well have I equipped my people to process their concerns or questions about how I am leading?
4. Am I perceived as approachable (do I invite people into my life to give feedback, or do people sense I will respond negatively if they share their concerns)?
5. Do I have the courage to eliminate patterns of gossip and grumbling in our ministry?

PRACTICAL STEPS TO CONSIDER

1. **Train your people how to process disagreements or negative feelings they have about what is happening in church** – There are few things more important to the relational health of a ministry than the people having good training and modeling in how to manage problems. Many church attendees come from poor family backgrounds and do not know how to do relationships well. It is the wise leader who is proactive in teaching relationship and conflict resolution skills that emphasize honor and the principles taught in Matthew 18:15-17.

2. **Refuse to be a dumping ground for those with critical attitudes** – If we tolerate constant negativity being spoken to us, it will keep on happening. Instead of passively or angrily receiving other people's garbage, we can tell people what they are to do if they have a disagreement with your leadership or others.

3. **Have a plan to overcome any unhealthy need you have for the approval of people** – You can lessen your desire for the praise of people by implementing the following: a) Get healed of your insecurities. b) Understand every leader has to learn how to overcome being criticized by others. c) Keep moving forward in your life because people who are growing are less likely to dwell on what people think of them. d) Learn to laugh at yourself and at the lie that you cannot have the joy of the Lord when there are people who are unhappy with you.

DECLARATIONS

- My people love and trust me because I have their best interests at heart.
- Every dysfunction in my ministry is being transformed into a strength.
- I have life-giving boundaries and protocols in my ministry which greatly eliminate strongholds of negativity.

5

SCENARIO

Ralph Respect pastors Let's Change the World Church. He has read books on honor and is frustrated because his people do not honor him as he thinks they should. He sees other pastors receiving honor, but his people do nothing special for him on Pastor Appreciation Sunday or any other time of year. He teaches on honor, but he does not think the people understand it. If you were Ralph, what would you do?

LIES ASSOCIATED WITH THIS SCENARIO

- I am the only leader in the world who feels dishonored by those they lead.
- I must demand that people honor me.
- If my people don't honor me now, they will never honor me.
- I am unworthy of honor.

LIFE AND LEADERSHIP CORE VALUES TO CONSIDER

45 I give generously in the areas where I have need.
48 My response to something is almost always more important than the something.
51 I focus more on heart connections than outward obedience toward those I lead.
71 I take the "log" out of my own eye before trying to take the speck out of someone else's eye.
78 There is a designated person or persons who help the people of our church know how to treat a pastor.

DISCERNING WHAT GOD IS DEVELOPING IN ME

- I am learning to prosper on the inside when things are not what I want them to be on the outside.
- I have the opportunity to evaluate the true source of my feelings.
- I get to inspire people to walk in greater honor.

QUESTIONS TO ASK BEFORE TAKING ACTION

- Am I modeling the type of honor I want the people to have?
- Do any of my behaviors and attitudes hinder people's ability to honor me?
- What trusted person can I share my concern with to get feedback?
- Am I willing to serve people even if they don't honor me as I think they should?
- What do other pastors do about this issue?

PRACTICAL STEPS TO CONSIDER

1. **Model honor and eliminate obvious behaviors which hinder people from honoring you** – If you desire more honor, increase the honor you give to all people (especially those who are over you in ministry). Who you are will influence your people much more than what you say. If you are dishonoring in speech and attitude toward those you disagree with or who have hurt you, then it is unlikely people will increase their heart of honor for you. Besides getting rid of dishonor in your own life, eliminate these other "honor killers" for pastors: victim mentalities, blatant hypocrisy, unwillingness to admit mistakes, putting "guilt trips" on people to motivate them, and letting people become too familiar with you.

2. **Enlist someone to teach your people how to treat a pastor** – Ideally, this person is a leader in the church, but it can also be a regular guest speaker or other outside influencer. This equipper of the people needs to be respected and able to cast vision for stewarding relationship with the senior pastor well, not someone who uses guilt and condemnation as tools to motivate. It is not selfish for the senior leader to strategize with people like this to get such a plan, but it is a step of wisdom for the overall health of the church.

3. **Overcome any disappointment or codependency you have with those you lead** – Growing leaders do not assess the quality of their lives by how their people treat them, but by having a word from the Lord and by having a great assignment in their hearts (Matthew 4:4, Nehemiah 6:3). They love people but are not dependent upon their approval to thrive in life. They also have received grace to overcome the tendency to be chronically disappointed in their flock (forgiving from the heart).

DECLARATIONS

- I live a life of great honor which causes the people of my church to honor everyone including me.
- My people know how to treat a pastor well.
- My people respect me as their leader.

SCENARIO

Rockin' and Rollin' Church in Loud, Louisiana loves worship. Their services usually last about one hour and thirty minutes with worship consisting of an hour of the time. Harry Hearing regularly comes up to Pastor Rick Rocker and complains about the music being too loud. He also says that many other people share the same opinion. Pastor Rocker believes that his church is called to prolonged worship. Rick isn't sure what to do with this feedback as he believes that the music is at the perfect volume. If you were Pastor Rocker, what would you do?

LIES ASSOCIATED WITH THIS SCENARIO

- My goal as the pastor is to make sure everyone in church likes our worship volume and style.
- People who say the music is too loud are always wrong.
- If I turn the music down, the worship team will be offended and the worship will not be as anointed.
- The only two people who should decide how loud the music should be are the worship leader and the sound person.

LIFE AND LEADERSHIP CORE VALUES TO CONSIDER

8   I pursue "buy-in" from leaders and key people involved before making a big decision.
10 I create opportunities for those in my church to encounter God in powerful ways.
9   I build a culture of feedback in my ministry that I lead by example.
52 I am a God-pleaser, not a people-pleaser.
17 I thrive in uncertainty, difficulty, and unresolved situations because I have a "word" from the Lord.

DISCERNING WHAT GOD IS DEVELOPING IN ME

- I am learning how to help our worship department to go to the next level of excellence.
- I have the opportunity to really hear the concerns of the people in our church.
- I get to realize that not everyone will agree with me, and it is okay.

HELP! I'M A PASTOR

QUESTIONS TO ASK BEFORE TAKING ACTION

1. Is this the opinion of one person or the opinion of my church?
2. How can I better communicate our vision for our worship style?
3. How can I send the "I value you" message to those who are concerned?
4. Have I used a decibel sound meter to see if the noise level is at all dangerous?
5. What have other churches I respect done about this?

PRACTICAL STEPS TO CONSIDER

1. **Set a decibel level for worship and stick with it** – Buy a decibel sound meter (also available in apps for your phone) and have your sound team trained in how to use it. Get your worship team on board as well. Record sound levels for a few weeks. (The sound is louder during practice, because the room is empty). Find the best decibel level for your room (it will vary from location to location because of factors such as size, acoustics, echoes, etc.). Set a maximum level, but leave yourself some flexibility for a powerful lift in a song without blowing out someone's eardrums. This will obviously work a lot better if the sound technicians are honored people in your ministry and are trained well.

2. **Respond to the complaint with good questions and suggestions** – It is unwise to simply get irritated with those who express concern about the music volume. Here are some questions you can kindly ask: a) "Was it louder than usual?" b) "Was there a song that was particularly loud?" c) "Where were you sitting?" At times, people will have a legitimate complaint that needs addressing. Two practical ways to help would be to suggest a different seat or to provide ear plugs for them.

3. **Learn how to address situations with proactivity, wisdom, and humor** – a) Build toward agreement of philosophy by sharing "seed thoughts" (brief truths) in sermons. b) Share a clear vision about worship. c) Personally pursue heart connection with the most concerned. d) Use humor in messages to help people understand their opinion is one of many – and that there are others who encourage you in the opposite direction. e) Instill vision for all the key people (sound person, worship team, ushers, etc.) to be on the same page in philosophy and in graciousness to those who complain.

DECLARATIONS

- I value people and their opinions without compromising core values.
- I always look for opportunities to grow and to take things to the next level.
- We have outstanding sound technicians and worship leaders in our ministry.

SCENARIO

Two key leaders, Ray Zingkane and Holden D. Grudge, met for breakfast to plan the upcoming giving campaign. After five minutes, it was obvious that they had two completely different approaches to raising money. Ray said that Holden was unspiritual and had no faith. Holden responded that Ray had his head in the clouds and needed to be realistic. The meal ended with Ray Zingkane storming out angrily and making a bit of a scene. It has been three weeks since they have spoken. Many in the church feel the tension and know what is going on. What should you as the senior leader do?

LIES ASSOCIATED WITH THIS SCENARIO

- My church must not be a safe place if there is conflict.
- Disagreements in the church are always a bad thing.
- I do not have the wisdom or authority to confront people to help them resolve their discord.
- No successful church has ever had conflict between its leaders.

LIFE AND LEADERSHIP CORE VALUES TO CONSIDER

9 I build a culture of feedback in my ministry that I lead by example.
41 I decrease gossip in our ministry by setting the example of speaking directly with the people that I have a problem with and inviting them to speak directly with me.
58 I confront people with love and inspire them to grow by reminding them of their destiny.
76 I purpose to communicate sensitive matters with people face to face and not through text or email.
77 My ministry provides regular training and education on key life skills.

DISCERNING WHAT IS BEING DEVELOPED IN ME

- I am learning to partner with the Holy Spirit in understanding how to help people overcome relational conflict.
- I have the opportunity to practice love at a new level.
- I get to grow in having God help me master the art of confronting with honor.

QUESTIONS TO ASK BEFORE TAKING ACTION

1. Is my timing and heart right to get involved?
2. What can I do to better equip our church to be successful in relationships?
3. Am I am able to be objective in this situation, or do I have a bias that might get in the way of bringing restoration?
4. What other factors may be contributing to this relational difficulty?
5. How can this situation make me a better leader?

PRACTICAL STEPS TO CONSIDER

1. **"Keep your love on" if you believe you are to confront the situation** – The key to confrontation in a situation like this is that they feel you care about them as much as you care about solving the issue. Confrontation is a loving effort to show someone face to face what they might not see or know about how they are affecting the environment. You are there to turn the light on in the situation. You are letting them know, "You are way too awesome to be acting like this." (Danny Silk has an excellent chapter called "Kingdom Confrontation" in *Culture of Honor*. His book, *Keep Your Love On*, will also be helpful to you).

2. **Get the two people in a room together** – Eventually the two leaders need to meet in person and be reconciled. It is good to continue to encourage them to do this even if they are stubborn. You will know repentance has taken place when they are willing to clean up their mess. If they refuse, they need to understand that you cannot have leaders in the church who refuse to forgive.

3. **Ask good questions** – Spiritual "surgery" requires a scalpel, not a machete. People typically respond better to confrontation if they have given their permission for it before receiving it. We need to find the real root of the problem and make sure they take ownership of their problems. Here are some key questions to use in that process: a) I have noticed something about you. Can we talk about it? b) This is what I see… Can you help me understand? c) What are you going to do? d) How can I help? e) When can we follow up?

DECLARATIONS

- I affect my environments rather than being affected by them.
- I love and honor others regardless of how they respond to me.
- I consistently turn conflict into kingdom growth for others and myself.

6

PASTOR OR FRIEND? CAN I BE BOTH WITH MY PEOPLE?

SCENARIO

Pastor Conn Ection is the new senior leader at Heart Connection Center Church. He is an extroverted person who likes to outwardly process what is going on in his life. Perf, his wife, is more introverted and can only take so much of Conn's need to share what is going on in his life, Conn is concerned he will not have sufficient quality relationships in this new season of life and ministry. This apprehension was heightened when he heard one of his denominational leaders say that the pastor should never be "buddy buddy" with the people of his church. Conn wonders if it is wise to become good friends with some of the men of his new church. If you were Pastor Conn, what would you do?

LIES ASSOCIATED WITH THIS SCENARIO

- Only one personality type can be successful as a pastor.
- Pastors need to stay distant from their people so the members of the congregation will not see any of their weaknesses.
- Leaders are only worthy of double honor (1 Timothy 5:17) if it is obvious they deserve it.
- A pastor should not be concerned about becoming too friendly with the people of the church.

LIFE AND LEADERSHIP CORE VALUES TO CONSIDER

7   My team and I pursue spiritual fathers and mothers we mutually respect.
20 I proactively anticipate challenges that could occur in the future.
40 I live with intentionality by having a clear set of priorities, which dictate how I spend my time.
51 I focus more on heart connections than outward obedience toward those I lead.
16 I embrace seasons of building trust in the eyes of those I lead.

DISCERNING WHAT GOD IS DEVELOPING IN ME

- I am learning the balance of being friends with those in my ministry while not letting those friendships create "favorites" in my ministry setting.
- I have the opportunity to develop my philosophy about what is appropriate and what is not appropriate concerning the relationships I have with those I lead.
- I get to develop a quality plan for the relationships in my life.

QUESTIONS TO ASK BEFORE TAKING ACTION

1. Do I understand the potential problems my personality type can have regarding relationships in the church?
2. Who do I have outside of this ministry that I can open up to about what is happening in my life and ministry?
3. What type of things should I avoid sharing with someone I am leading?
4. Is the fear of man holding me back from having quality relationships with some of the people I am leading?
5. Have I taught my people the philosophy I have regarding my friendships in the church?

PRACTICAL STEPS TO CONSIDER

1. **Find a group of people "to do life with"** – Pastors and their families need to do life with others (especially if they have children in the home). Those we do life with will usually be in our own church, and often in our leadership team. These relationships are beneficial for many reasons. They help us to have the friendships we need and they allow people to see how we do life – both to learn from us and to understand where we need support from others.

2. **Develop friendships with the people you lead, but do not have favorites** – We should not isolate ourselves from our people, but we also cannot have "teachers' pets" in our ministry. We may spend more time with particular people, but that reality cannot create a favoritism toward them.

3. **Recognize the pitfalls of your people becoming "too familiar" with you** – There are two extremes in relationships with the people of your church. The first extreme is to be so separated from the people that no one really gets to know you; this could subconsciously create an unrealistic view of who you are. The other extreme is to be so "buddy buddy" with the people that your authority is weakened. Just as parents must be careful to live in a way that causes their children to respect them, so must church leaders.

DECLARATIONS

- I have great relationships with the people of my church.
- I am respected and loved by those I lead.
- I clearly know how close I should be with the people in my church.

7

HOW TRANSPARENT IS TOO TRANSPARENT?

SCENARIO

Pastor I. M. Authentic hates hypocrisy and phoniness. He is one of those people who feels insincere if he just answers "fine" to the question, "How are you doing?" He wants people to know he battles what they battle. He at times says things that make people cringe, but Pastor Authentic usually believes it is their problem, not his. Lately, he has been questioning how transparent he should be, especially after he revealed something in a sermon which embarrassed his teenage son. Pastor Authentic is walking the line between being authentic and oversharing. If you were him, what would you do?

LIES ASSOCIATED WITH THIS SCENARIO

- I am a hypocrite unless I tell everyone I am leading about every struggle I have.
- The only way I can be respected is if my people think I do not have any weaknesses.
- My wife and family are wrong to get upset if I share about our family struggles.
- Humility comes before a fall, but pride brings honor.

LIFE AND LEADERSHIP CORE VALUES TO CONSIDER

51 I focus more on heart connections than outward obedience toward those I lead.
49 I am "sent" by trustworthy people into the ministry I have, and I continue to pursue personal accountability with them.
52 I am a God-pleaser, not a people-pleaser.
25 I believe people's negative qualities are usually immature characteristics of positive qualities in their life.
74 I have at least one person in my life with whom I share the deep things of my life with (things such as disappointments, weaknesses, dreams, fears, and longings).

DISCERNING WHAT GOD IS DEVELOPING IN ME

- I am learning to understand the weakness within one of my greatest strengths.
- I have the opportunity to see in a greater way how others perceive me.
- I get to increase my sensitivity to others (especially my family) when I share intimate details of my life.

QUESTIONS TO ASK BEFORE TAKING ACTION

1. How would I counsel other pastors on how transparent they should be?
2. Do my family members and close people in my life feel like I will protect their feelings and reputation in what I say?
3. Do I have someone I trust who gives me feedback after I speak? If not, who can?
4. How can I encourage more healthy transparency in our ministry?
5. What else is God saying to me about this?

PRACTICAL STEPS TO CONSIDER

1. **Recognize the pitfalls of sharing too much or too little with your church** – It is a good thing to understand whether you tend to share too much or too little. If you reveal too much, it can create questions in people's minds about whether you are someone they want to follow (especially for those who don't know your heart). If you are too private and/or give the impression you don't battle common life struggles, then hope levels and heart connections will be weak in the ministry.

2. **Mainly share about battles you have already won or are winning** – Biblical teaching must have a practical application, and our testifying how we are living those truths out in normal areas of life is powerful. As we reveal our imperfections, we help people understand how to celebrate progress and not just perfection. There will also be times in ministry when we open up to our people (or to our core group) about a current situation that we don't have the victory in yet. These times should not be the norm, but they allow us to send "I need you" messages to our people, which is key for deeper connections.

3. **Create a sense of safety in your congregation by prioritizing your family** – "In the multitude of words sin is not lacking, but he who restrains his lips is wise" (Proverbs 10:19). If we talk a lot or are an outward processor, we will be prone to say things we should not say. If we expose people's weakness in messages or conversations, not only are those talked about going to struggle with us, but it will also make people wonder if we will protect them in future public or personal conversations. Our restraint in speech is a key for people to conclude we are safe leaders. Begin by restraining from telling in-depth family details.

DECLARATIONS

- My words constantly release life.
- My humility and transparency are powerful aspects of my ministry.
- The people of our ministry know I will protect their dignity in what I say.

SCENARIO

Senior Pastor O. Vern Whelmed loves people, enjoys preaching, and brings incredible breakthrough to people through his ministry. He comes alive through these things, but unexpected administrative duties drain him. Last Sunday, things reached a breaking point for Pastor Whelmed. At 6:00 AM he received a text saying his sound person would not be in service. When he arrived at church at 7:30, he noticed the church was not clean and the bulletins were not done. After taking care of these matters, the service started and he tried to worship, but he saw that the wrong song was put on the screen during worship. Then Unis Unhinged came to him saying, "God has told me if I go on the stage now and yell 'Shabba shabba,' the glory will fall." After Pastor Whelmed dispatched Unis, Elder Thomas Thorny came up and said, "Pastor, the music is too loud!" If you were Pastor O. Vern, what would you do?

LIES ASSOCIATED WITH THIS SCENARIO

*   There are no solutions for this.
*   Administration only hinders revival.
*   All the problems that are being experienced are an attack of the devil.
*   The only way to thrive in ministry is if everything goes perfectly in meetings and in the church.

LIFE AND LEADERSHIP CORE VALUES TO CONSIDER

48 My response to something is almost always more important than the something.
13 I refuse to blame those I lead for the quality of our ministry.
20 I proactively anticipate challenges that could occur in the future.
17 I thrive in uncertainty, difficulty, and unresolved situations because I have a "word" from the Lord.
51 I focus more on heart connections than outward obedience toward those I lead.

DISCERNING WHAT GOD IS DEVELOPING IN ME

*   I am learning to prioritize the administrative aspect of the ministry.
*   I have the opportunity to inspire others to a higher level of faithfulness and commitment.
*   I get to have a prosperous soul when in chaotic circumstances.

QUESTIONS TO ASK BEFORE TAKING ACTION

1. Have my leadership team and I asked the Holy Spirit what is to be done?
2. Can I create an intern program that would be a win-win for the intern and me?
3. Have I prayed and believed for an administrative assistant?
4. What areas do I believe I need to grow in concerning administration?
5. How much money should we devote to administration?

PRACTICAL STEPS TO CONSIDER

1. **Take steps to grow in your administrative abilities** – Scripture says we have a sound mind (2 Timothy 1:7), and we have the Creator of the universe living inside us. This truth lets us know we have the ability to plan and organize well. Yes, some of us have not been trained in the basics of time management, people management, productivity, and how to adequately prepare for upcoming events, but these are things we can grow in by upgrading our beliefs and by giving time to them.

2. **Prioritize your relationship with administrative people in your ministry** – "But now God has set the members, each one of them, in the body just as He pleased" (1 Corinthians 12:18). You can be confident God has or will set vital administrative people in your midst. It might be your spouse, or it could be someone you have overlooked. Remember, what you celebrate in your ministry will attract more people to that emphasis. It is the wise leader who honors those with administrative gifts in the church so more will be drawn in.

3. **Ignite your people with vision for being faithful and growing in excellence** – You have two main ways to motivate your people. One is by the law – "You are a bad Christian unless you do these things." The other is through vision – "You are being prepared for something greater. As you are faithful in what is least, God will open doors for you into greater influence and experiences in Him." As you grow in this as a leader, it will lessen your administrative headaches.

DECLARATIONS

- Our ministry walks in great excellence.
- I thrive in ministry even when we experience administrative breakdowns in our midst.
- We have powerful administrative people who contribute significantly in our church.

SCENARIO

Reba Ryechuz has had some bad experiences with Tarry Jones. Tarry is on the altar prayer team and also stands on the stage as an intercessor during worship. Reba feels Tarry is a hypocrite who is nice in public (especially when pastor, Andy Advancer, is near), but treats people with disrespect and haughtiness. Reba tells Pastor Advancer, "Tarry is a Jezebel. She looks good on the outside, but is full of darkness on the inside. You should not have someone like this representing your church in ministry." If you were Pastor Advancer, what would you do?

LIES ASSOCIATED WITH THIS SCENARIO

- I should not use anyone in ministry who is disliked by one or more church attendees.
- God would never warn me about a person through someone like Reba.
- When I hear someone speak negatively about another person, I should think less of that person immediately.
- As long as a person is anointed in a church service, it does not matter what choices or attitudes he or she has outside of the ministry setting.

LIFE AND LEADERSHIP CORE VALUES TO CONSIDER

31   Those who regularly influence our ministry are known and trusted.

41   I decrease gossip in our ministry by setting the example of speaking directly with the people that I have a problem with and inviting them to speak directly with me.

27   I process unverified information about others in a healthy way.

58   I confront people with love and inspire them to grow by reminding them of their destiny.

67   The people of our ministry have clear, healthy avenues for them to share concerns they have about the church or me.

DISCERNING WHAT GOD IS DEVELOPING IN ME

- I am learning how to equip my people to have high standards in how they process concerns they have with others in the church.
- I have the opportunity to avoid making conclusions about people based on hearsay or bitterness from others.
- I get to re-evaluate the standards I have for those who minister.

QUESTIONS TO ASK BEFORE TAKING ACTION

1. What is my relationship with the one who is making the Jezebel accusation and how should my leadership team and I respond to her?
2. Is it clear how our people should handle concerns they have about others?
3. How well do the leadership team and I know those who minister in our church?
4. How can we help these two to strengthen their relationship?
5. Is this accusation important enough to investigate?

PRACTICAL STEPS TO CONSIDER

1. **Determine to not have "knee jerk" reactions to an individual's comments about others** – It is not infrequent for leaders to hear negative comments about people in their ministry. This can range from someone expressing a simple concern or it can be an angry attack. Unless the negative report has serious implications (e.g. someone is being abused or someone is in danger), it is prudent to refrain from impulsive responses. It is best to give the benefit of the doubt before proceeding into any action.

2. **Be proactive in strengthening the relationships between the people in your ministry** – Church leaders cannot be concerned just about their own relationships with their congregation, but also must give attention to the interpersonal relationships of the people in the ministry. Two ways to do this are through raising up pastoral influencers and through consistent prayer. Relational breakdowns can also be lessened in the church by regular training on relationships and conflict resolution (including clear steps for people to take to address concerns they have with others).

3. **Give people valuable information to help relieve their anxiety about what is happening** – It is good to teach your congregation how you think when someone reports negative information to you about another. Let them know: a) You err on the side of believing too much in people (as they would want you to do about them). b) You believe character and integrity are vital for leadership roles. c) You are not afraid to confront people who are clearly doing wrong. d) You are working with your leadership team to strengthen the lives of everyone who ministers publicly in any way.

DECLARATIONS

- I process information given to me about others in a healthy way.
- The people in my ministry walk in honor and wisdom in their relationships.
- Our ministry is free from gossip and focuses on building each other up.

10   "PASTOR, YOUR SERMONS DON'T FEED ME"

SCENARIO

After Pastor B.D. Word preached on a Sunday morning, a member of his church, I.M. Famished, approached him. "Pastor, I have loved being here, but your sermons just aren't feeding me. This is my last Sunday here. I am going to look for another church." Pastor B.D. Word was shocked and hurt. He didn't know whether to laugh nervously, get defensive, or quit the ministry. If you were Pastor Word, how would you respond?

LIES ASSOCIATED WITH THIS SCENARIO

- Because I received negative feedback, I must not be called to preach or teach.
- This person is just a consumer Christian and needs to learn to feed themselves.
- If someone isn't happy, I must be doing something wrong.
- There is nothing I need to improve in my preaching or teaching style.

LIFE AND LEADERSHIP CORE VALUES TO CONSIDER

9   I build a culture of feedback in my ministry that I lead by example.
13   I refuse to blame those I lead for the quality of our ministry.
14   I am more concerned about building people than I am concerned about building a ministry.
44   I seek to listen and understand before I seek to be heard and understood.
48   My response to something is almost always more important than the something.

DISCERNING WHAT IS BEING DEVELOPED IN ME

- I am learning to get my identity and self-worth from God, not the affirmation or criticism of people.
- I have the opportunity for God to grow me as a communicator of His Word.
- I get to grow to be "quick to listen, slow to speak, and slow to anger" (James 1:19) when someone says something that stings.

QUESTIONS TO ASK BEFORE TAKING ACTION

1. Is this an isolated incident or consistent feedback that I get?
2. What do the people I trust most say about my speaking ability?
3. How does God feel about this situation?
4. Am I preaching "the whole counsel of God" (Acts 20:27)?
5. Am I putting time and prayer into my messages or giving "stale" leftovers?

PRACTICAL STEPS TO CONSIDER

1. **Make sure your sermons are an overflow from your life with God** – We teach what we know. We impart who we are. We can not give what we do not have. Jack Hayford said this about preparing sermons: "If it feeds you, it will feed them." Bill Johnson has said, "I never study to prepare a sermon. I study for me. When I teach, I am breaking off a piece of my own life and feeding them." What are the relationships, experiences, and practices that feed your heart? If you are not encountering the Lord or having the message hit you at some point during your preparation, nobody else will either. Is your schedule or pace of life affecting your sermon preparation or your alone time with God? If so, you may need to delegate more responsibility or recruit more volunteers or staff.

2. **Create a strategy to grow and develop as a communicator of God's Word** – There is a saying, "All Word and no Spirit, you dry up. All Spirit and no Word, you blow up. Word and Spirit together, you grow up." Learn how to partner with the Holy Spirit to see God's anointing change people's lives through your messages. Also, constantly seek to improve your public speaking skills by taking classes, studying other communicators, reading books that inspire you, and/or participating in a group that inspires people to grow in delivering sermons.

3. **Gracefully bless the transition of the one leaving the church** – Remember, they are not "our" people, but they are God's people. If someone feels they are not being fed, allow them to transition gracefully. Use the "grocery store test" to help you know how to respond. You want to be able to see that person in the grocery store and be able to go up to them and say hello and not have to go down another aisle to avoid them. As church leaders, our heart is to see people grow. If they will grow in the Lord more at another church, then we should bless them to go.

DECLARATIONS

- When I speak, the Holy Spirit rides upon my words and transforms lives.
- I am committed to continually improving my preaching and teaching.
- I respond well when people criticize me.

SCENARIO

A very popular leader in the church, Evan Jelist, comes to his senior pastor, R. U. Fild, and says, "I feel called to plant a church that will primarily focus on reaching lost people. God has even opened up a building for this five miles from here!" Pastor Fild is uncomfortable with the news and even questions himself whether this is disloyal or dishonoring. He has big dreams for Evan at his church. What would you do?

LIES ASSOCIATED WITH THIS SCENARIO

- If this church plant opens close to us, we are going to lose all of our people.
- I have every right to be angry and fearful about this situation.
- I must be doing something wrong for someone from our church to want to plant another church in our city.
- There are not enough people in our city for another church.

LIFE AND LEADERSHIP CORE VALUES TO CONSIDER

14 I am more concerned about building people than I am concerned about building a ministry.
24 My leaders and I frequently ask the question, "What is the Holy Spirit saying to us?"
42 I am primarily a developer of leaders.
50 I believe people want to do the right thing; therefore, my default belief is to give the benefit of the doubt to others.
53 I help people understand how their behavior impacts others.

DISCERNING WHAT GOD IS DEVELOPING IN ME

- I am learning the calling and destiny of our church, so I will not be moved when key people move on.
- I have the opportunity to trust God, not myself, to build the church.
- I get to prioritize having a heart for the overall body of Christ.

QUESTIONS TO ASK BEFORE TAKING ACTION

1. Is the Holy Spirit stirring something here?
2. Is this the right timing for this church plant?
3. Am I reacting as a father or in fear?
4. What do people I trust say about this potential plant?
5. What concerns do I have about this situation that need to be addressed?

PRACTICAL STEPS TO CONSIDER

1. **Establish a "safe place" for them to discuss this openly and honestly with you** – If the Holy Spirit is prompting this, you want to follow Him even if it feels uncomfortable. Thank the person for coming to you. Encourage them to follow the prompting of the Holy Spirit wherever He leads. Offer to support them in any way that you can, without over-promising anything. If you need time to take it all in, ask for some time to "marinate" on the discussion and set up a future time to talk. Use this time to check your own heart for anything that isn't from God. Make sure they have sought wise counsel from other spiritual fathers and mothers in their life. (Many church splits have occurred because a church wouldn't release people who had a vision that was different enough from theirs, or if they were not willing to find a way to accomplish it together.) If after time you do not feel this is God, you need to share your apprehensions with them – whether it is timing, character, or other concerns.

2. **Announce their departure** – Realize how you handle announcing this departure will either build or hinder trust in your church and your leadership. If you feel you are to bless this departure and you do it well, this transition will help the congregation see your empowering leadership and will build a culture of honor. Done poorly, it can make the senior leaders look controlling and fearful. Before sharing anything publicly, make sure key people are informed. Allow plenty of time for those affected to prepare for the transition. Let the church planters leave graciously so they can come back without shame if needed.

3. **Protect the relationship as you move forward** – The heart of a father wants their sons and daughters to surpass them in every area. Fathers believe something about their kids that they cannot believe about themselves. One reflection of these strong beliefs is to refrain from speaking negatively about this person to others. Also, to solidify the protection of this relationship, pray for a smooth transition that deepens the honor between everyone involved.

DECLARATIONS

- God works all things together for good in my ministry.
- As we release people to go, we receive greater multiplication back to us.
- Our church is a leadership engine that produces an abundance of leaders for every sphere of society.

Note: We are mainly addressing mindsets of pastors in this scenario. To those who are considering planting a church near their current church – we would urge great caution in proceeding with this if this step would potentially cause division or a church split.

SCENARIO

After a series of sensitive conversations among the leadership team, you notice one of your younger leaders, Dee Vulge, posting comments on her Facebook wall that relate to the sensitive topics at hand. Allusions are made about the actions of people, which sound very familiar to ones on your leadership team. While you notice the increasing response to these posts, you realize that this is becoming gossip and stirring up division. How do you approach Dee regarding her usage of social media?

LIES ASSOCIATED WITH THIS SCENARIO

- If I confront her about it, that would be controlling and dishonoring to her.
- It is not that big of a deal for a leader to publicly share everything that happens in important meetings.
- That was a bad hire, and I should quickly make changes in her responsibilities.
- Social media is from the devil and cannot be beneficial.

LIFE AND LEADERSHIP CORE VALUES TO CONSIDER

53   I help people understand how their behavior impacts others.
79   I realize the same environment that exposed a Judas also created eleven world changers.
63   Freedom does not mean that anything can happen.
58   I confront people with love and inspire them to grow by reminding them of their destiny.
44   I seek to listen and understand before I seek to be heard and understood.

DISCERNING WHAT GOD IS DEVELOPING IN ME

- I am learning to love individuals even when there is disagreement.
- I have the opportunity to restore relationships to peace.
- I get to improve my ability to confront people in a healthy way.

QUESTIONS TO ASK BEFORE TAKING ACTION

1. How have I protected the unity of our team amidst conflict?
2. Am I prepared to listen, to understand, and to extend grace as I hear how this individual's hurt may be leading to such a reaction?
3. Am I prepared to walk this person into wholeness if there is repentance?
4. Which well-respected leader on our team could help bring resolution to this?
5. What wisdom might we share with our people regarding the use of social media?

PRACTICAL STEPS TO CONSIDER

1. **Get a plan for the do's and dont's of social media** – It is wisdom to address this. Social media is likely a big part of the lives of most people who attend your church. Young and old need to be warned about what they post – whether it is personal information, gossip, inappropriate humor, pictures that negatively impact your Christian witness, or venting about something you disagree with. Besides these warnings, communicate that social media more importantly provides opportunities to love people, share the gospel, and inform others of testimonies and the good things that are happening.

2. **Strengthen your training to help people handle disagreements in a healthy way** – Do not assume that new leaders understand how to process frustrations and disagreements about you or what is happening in the ministry. One of the most important things we can do for the future health of the church is to equip people to use the Matthew 18:15-17 principle of going directly to people they are having problems with. This principle is made easier for people if we are approachable and accountable in our leadership.

3. **Take your leadership meetings to the next level** – Here are some ideas to include in leadership meetings which will lessen the chance of gossip and lingering frustration afterward: a) Have an agenda. b) Follow-up on things from previous meetings. c) Share testimonies about good things in the church. d) Take time to encourage, thank, and prophesy over a leader at each meeting. e) Note who might be struggling with things and personally follow-up with them later. f) Give opportunities in meetings for people to express concerns or questions. g) Make sure strong personalities do not continually dominate conversations.

DECLARATIONS

*   My people are positioned for breakthrough in every area of their lives.
*   Every conversation I have points people closer to Christ and sets them up for life-changing love encounters with God.
*   The people I lead leverage social media in a healthy way to effectively advance the mission of the ministry.

SCENARIO

Pastor Ned Helps has a church of 100 people. One of his members, Phil Thuneed, has been voluntarily doing children's ministry every week. Phil mentioned recently that he is feeling burnt out and desiring to serve elsewhere. The last volunteer that expressed interest did not show up. For the last four months, no one has responded to the verbal requests for help in children's ministry. Pastor Helps is faced with a tough situation. He doesn't know how to relieve Phil and still have this ministry continue without him. What would you do?

LIES ASSOCIATED WITH THIS SCENARIO

- If I ask for help in the church too much, people will get annoyed and stop coming to church.
- Children's ministry is only a stepping stone to real ministry.
- Anyone who does not want to serve in our children's ministry is a bad Christian.
- I am not an empowering enough leader to inspire people to want to help in children's ministry.

LIFE AND LEADERSHIP CORE VALUES TO CONSIDER

8   I pursue "buy in" from leaders and key people involved before making a big decision.
42   I am primarily a developer of leaders.
66   I motivate people through vision instead of guilt and manipulation.
69   Children do not have a junior Holy Spirit.
45   I give generously in the areas where I have need.

DISCERNING WHAT GOD IS DEVELOPING IN ME

- I am learning how to create a culture that values the next generation and is excited to invest in them.
- I have the opportunity to inspire, raise up, and equip new leaders for children's ministry.
- I get to believe in a greater way that the Lord will provide for all my needs and those of my people.

HELP! I'M A PASTOR

QUESTIONS TO ASK BEFORE TAKING ACTION

1. Who on our leadership team can I strategize a plan with?
2. What are five things I can do to create greater vision for children's ministry?
3. What are other churches doing that is working?
4. Have I realized and responded to the main reasons people do not want to serve?
5. How could we pay for a part time person to lead this ministry?

PRACTICAL STEPS TO CONSIDER

1. **Personally lead a meeting for parents of children and others interested in children's ministry** – Here is an idea that will help bring breakthrough in any area of need in the church: Call a meeting for people who have a heart for a particular ministry. Lead this meeting as the senior leader (unless your church is large enough to have another leader lead). Share your heart with the group. Take time to pray about this need. Ask the Holy Spirit to speak. Let people share what they believe God is saying. Discuss strategies. Conclude on an action step or steps. Meet again in a few months. Through these meetings, identify those with integrity, who are passionate, and have your core values to be on a team to help in the ministry.

2. **Move forward in becoming a church parents want to attend** – Some practical steps include: a) Clean up the nursery. b) Have a family pastor. c) Support local schools. d) Have a Moms group. e) Include practical helps for families in sermons, blogs, social media, and in other ways. f) Have annual parenting classes and marriage training. g) Find ways to be a strength to single parents. Finally, don't underestimate the power of simply noticing and being kind to the children in your church. All parents love to be around those who think their kids are special.

3. **Do what you can now to see children powerfully impacted by the gospel** – Studies have shown most Christians came to faith as a child or were strongly influenced to do so from a childhood experience. Even if your children's ministry is struggling, there are things you can do to impact children: children's camps, Vacation Bible Schools, prayer meetings for children, after school clubs, special services for children, and having children participate in training for things such as praying for the sick. Find ways to bless and honor children during services.

DECLARATIONS

- I communicate about needs in my ministry with vision and inspiration.
- My high-level beliefs attract outstanding children's workers.
- The children of our church are the next world leaders. Signs and wonders follow them.

14 THE INCESSANT TALKER

SCENARIO

Pastor Vair E. Fair values interaction and input from people in meetings he leads. It usually has gone well in the past, but that was before Don Dominator started attending his church. Don has a very powerful personality, and he loves to talk. It is not unusual for him to go on ten-minute verbal marathons at home groups and in meetings – often taking the conversation off topic. Also, Mr. Dominator always seems to be the first person to speak in any group setting. People like Slowie Processor and Moses Stutterer never seem to get a word in when Don is in the room. If you were Pastor Fair, what would you do?

LIES ASSOCIATED WITH THIS SCENARIO

- People who talk too much cannot be a significant part of the church.
- There are no solutions concerning someone who loves to talk.
- If someone does not talk much, it means they have nothing important to say.
- I do not have the ability to lead meetings if there are strong personalities there.

LIFE AND LEADERSHIP CORE VALUES TO CONSIDER

9   I build a culture of feedback in my ministry that I lead by example.
20 I proactively anticipate challenges that could occur in the future.
22 I pursue relationships with the strong influencers in places I am called to lead.
25 I believe people's negative qualities are usually immature characteristics of positive qualities in their life.
53 I help people understand how their behavior impacts others.

DISCERNING WHAT GOD IS DEVELOPING IN ME

- I am learning how to lead small group meetings at a higher level.
- I have the opportunity to discern in a higher way how to have freedom without the same people dominating a meeting.
- I get to grow in inspiring and connecting with different personalities.

QUESTIONS TO ASK BEFORE TAKING ACTION

1. Is Don aware of his tendency to excessively talk?
2. How much training do we provide our leaders on leading small group meetings?
3. Is this situation exposing insecurities in me regarding me being a strong leader?
4. What can I learn from experienced small group leaders?
5. How can I structure meetings to avoid long-winded talkfests?

28

PRACTICAL STEPS TO CONSIDER

1. **Improve your leadership training on how to lead small groups** – Small group leadership training is a must for healthy experiences in these groups. This training should cover topics such as planning, building trust, nurturing growth, growing a leadership team, delegation, handling common problems, etc. There are many books and online resources to help with this. Also, it is good to have all small group leaders meet once or twice a year for a refresher training and to share with each other what is working and where they need help.

2. **Partner with the strong influencer to improve meetings** – One of the best strategies with any challenging person in group settings is to ask the person to partner with you to help the meeting flow better. This sends an "I need you" message to the person and helps him or her see the bigger picture. "Don, I love your enthusiasm to participate at such a high level in our small group. As you can probably see, people like Slowie and Moses don't share much. I want so much to help them grow in their confidence to share what God is giving them. Would you help me?"

3. **Learn how to decrease the likelihood of people regularly dominating meetings** – This can be done by: a) giving ground rules for what sharing will look like – "Keep your comments to two minutes or less," b) If the dominating person keeps talking, interrupt him as they catch their breath and say, "That's a good point. Slowie, what do you think?" c) If he interrupts someone who is talking, hold your hand up and say, "Sorry, Don, Moses was talking first." Turn to Moses and say, "Moses, now what were you saying?" d) Meet privately with the talker after the meeting to share in love what you saw happening and why you did what you did. Note: we need to be secure in our leadership. Our goal is not to prove to others we are a good leader but to actually believe we are a good leader.

DECLARATIONS

- My leaders and I are skilled facilitators of small group meetings.
- I really help incessant talkers know how to succeed in small groups.
- I am able to successfully lead different types of people.

15   PURSUING MIRACLES BUT FACING DISAPPOINTMENT

SCENARIO

Pastor B. Healed leads a charismatic church and believes in divine healing. However, she and her church are not seeing people healed. They have been pursuing healing like never before – sermon series, fasting, Bible studies, declarations – but no one is getting healed. In fact, one of their key church leaders recently died of a disease they were sure God would heal. Pastor B. Healed is tired of not seeing results and feels like giving up on healing. If you were Pastor Healed, how would you move forward?

LIES ASSOCIATED WITH THIS SCENARIO

- I do not have what it takes to lead this church into healing ministry.
- God is using sickness to build our character and teach us something.
- God has sovereignly chosen our church to not have a healing ministry.
- No one with a powerful healing ministry ever struggled at first to see healing.

LIFE AND LEADERSHIP CORE VALUES TO CONSIDER

7   My team and I pursue spiritual fathers and mothers we mutually respect.
10   I create opportunities for those in my church to encounter God in powerful ways.
17   I thrive in uncertainty, difficulty, and unresolved situations because I have a "word" from the Lord.
52   I am a God-pleaser, not a people-pleaser.
73   I intentionally associate with people who are stronger than me in key areas of life and ministry so I will become stronger in those areas.

DISCERNING WHAT GOD IS DEVELOPING IN ME

- I am learning perseverance that will serve me well when the breakthroughs come.
- I have the opportunity to receive an upgrade in my view of God.
- I get to grow in leading people into finding keys to seeing healing released.

QUESTIONS TO ASK BEFORE TAKING ACTION

1. Am I convinced it is God's will for us to walk in health? Do my doctrinal beliefs in any way limit what we are experiencing?
2. What are some things God is doing for me as I wait for breakthrough?
3. Who can I meet with that is seeing breakthrough in healing?
4. What healing Scriptures am I standing on that I know are true no matter what?

HELP! I'M A PASTOR

PRACTICAL STEPS TO CONSIDER

1. **Pursue the Healer, not just healing** – Do not let your pursuit of breakthrough distract you from the Lord of the breakthrough. Use this time to seek Him more than just the manifestation of healing. The more you know His heart, the easier it will be to believe Him for what Jesus paid for (Isaiah 53:5-6). God will not withhold healing from you because you are bad. He will not heal you because you are good. He will heal you because of what Jesus has done.

2. **Put yourself in environments where healing is happening** – Many things in the Spirit are better caught than taught. Consider being a part of a conference, healing school, and/or mission trip that focuses on activating believers in the supernatural and in healing. Many of these happenings have a time of impartation that can catalyze someone into more of the miraculous. Bill Johnson says, "If signs and wonders aren't following you, follow them until they follow you." If you connect with a speaker or group, consider bringing them to your church to activate and equip your people.

3. **Lead your church by example by taking risks and praying for people** – The culture of a church is shaped from the top down; so as you take risks, it will be imparted to your church. Some of the greatest healing revivalists prayed for hundreds of people before they saw someone healed. John Wimber taught on healing at his church every week for over two years before they saw their first person healed. There has to be a relentless tenacity when pursuing healing. Randy Clark says, "The price you pay for a healing ministry is to push past the disappointments." Remember: Healing is not our idea, healing is God's idea. We are not trying to convince Him. He is trying to convince us. When someone steps out and prays for someone, even if they do not experience healing, celebrate the risk, not just the testimony. Make sure to celebrate every testimony publicly.

DECLARATIONS
- Jesus is the same yesterday, today, and forever. He still likes to heal.
- I have authority to heal because of what Jesus has done.
- Our church is a magnet for healing, and people around us constantly get healed.

31

SCENARIO

Pastor Freddy Frustrated has a growing church and feels overwhelmed with details, needs, appointments, and sermon preparation – not to mention his personal growth and family life. He thinks that if he can just get someone else on staff, then some of the chaos will disappear. One of his board members, Penny Penshur, is not sure if the church can afford to pay another staff member, but Pastor Freddy believes the church can not afford not to. If you were Pastor Freddy, what would you do?

LIES ASSOCIATED WITH THIS SCENARIO

- A church should never do anything that would require faith.
- If we hire another person, the chaos and pressure will automatically go away.
- Penny is obviously an instrument of the devil and has no valid concerns.
- I should convince them that the only solution is to hire another staff member.

LIFE AND LEADERSHIP CORE VALUES TO CONSIDER

1 There is always a solution for every situation I face.
8 I pursue "buy-in" from leaders and key people involved before making a big decision.
19 I have a supernatural personal story as the basis for seemingly risky and illogical things I do.
32 I "date" people in key ministry relationships before "marrying" them with a title.
72 I interview the spouse of my potential key leaders.

DISCERNING WHAT GOD IS DEVELOPING IN ME

- I am learning the skills of leadership to recruit, train, release, and nurture leaders who multiply other leaders.
- I have the opportunity to grow in empowering volunteers.
- I get to lead my board into hearing God together on hiring decisions.

QUESTIONS TO ASK BEFORE TAKING ACTION

1. What will it cost us to hire this person? What will it cost us not to hire this person?
2. What is God saying about this solution? Am I just reacting to pressure?
3. Is there someone in our church who has shown faithfulness in smaller matters that is ready to lead in greater matters?
4. Is there a solution to meet this need aside from using the church's financial resources?

PRACTICAL STEPS TO CONSIDER

1. **Hire people who are "multipliers"** – Do not hire based on someone's promises of what they could do if they were hired, but look for those who are already contributing. Give people a "mina test" (Luke 19 – the test of faithfulness in smaller things leads to ruling cities). Look for those who are willing to sacrifice for a season who can produce those promises without being hired as paid staff. Look for leaders of leaders – those who make themselves irreplaceable by building teams and empowering people. You can hire less people when your staff empowers more church members.

2. **Look for the four C's: character, culture, competency, and chemistry** – *Character:* Let's assume everyone you are considering loves God and has good character. If not, cross them off of the list. *Culture:* Are they familiar with, and do they embrace, your culture? Getting this one right can make or break a team. Have they shown strong commitment to the vision of the church? This is much harder to determine if you are hiring from outside of your church. *Competency:* They may love God and have the culture, but can they do the job you need? *Chemistry:* When you think about spending time with this person, do you look forward to it? How will they work with other people on our team?

3. **Count the cost** – There are times when a church should step out in faith and hire another staff person. The key decision makers should feel that it is "right to us and the Holy Spirit" (Acts 15:28) – which implies those making the decision are connected to God's heart on the matter. Once hired, you and your board should work on a pay structure until you have a peace from the Holy Spirit regarding the fairness of the compensation. Some variables that will determine a pastor's or staff member's salary are size of the congregation, scope of responsibility, years of service, and special family needs. Empower all staff members to generate income outside of their church salary. Challenge them to pursue at least four streams of income. If there are current staff members who are ineffective, deal with them before adding new staff.

DECLARATIONS

- I attract and hire the best leaders on the planet for our mission and vision.
- God always shows up when we make hiring decisions.
- We have more than enough resources to accomplish our mission and help others accomplish theirs.

SCENARIO

Inclusive Church has lively church services led by Pastor B. Free. It is not unusual for someone in the congregation to share a prophetic word or to speak in a tongue and give an interpretation. This was not a problem for the first year of the church, but recently there have been awkward situations that have disrupted the flow of the service. One person stood up and prophesied that a certain politician was the anti-Christ. Furthermore, a new woman in church brings a tambourine and plays it loudly and off-beat. This causes problems for the worship team. If you were Pastor Free, what would you do?

LIES ASSOCIATED WITH THIS SCENARIO

*   I need to tightly control every meeting so nothing can go wrong.
*   I need to take the course of action which makes the fewest people angry.
*   I will quench the Spirit if I try to do something to stop the tambourine player.
*   I need to label the tambourine player and the "anti-Christ" prophesier as Jezebels who carry a religious spirit.

LIFE AND LEADERSHIP CORE VALUES TO CONSIDER

26 I err on the side of allowing too much Holy Spirit activity, rather than too little.
28 I regularly educate our people about our ministry's philosophy and process of decision making.
51 I focus more on heart connections than outward obedience toward those I lead.
31 Those who regularly influence our ministry are known and trusted.
61 I have high-level beliefs about the people I lead.

DISCERNING WHAT GOD IS DEVELOPING IN ME

*   I am learning to determine how much "body ministry" is healthy for our church.
*   I have the opportunity to determine what qualifications are needed for those who consistently influence the spiritual environment.
*   I get to grow in my brave communication skills.

QUESTIONS TO ASK BEFORE TAKING ACTION

1. What other times, besides the main service, could people have the opportunity to prophesy and play the tambourine?
2. Who is in relationship with these people who could help me get a greater heart connection with them?
3. How much of a disruption are these happenings?
4. What is there to celebrate in the life of the prophesier and tambourine player?
5. What have other ministries done about these types of happenings?

PRACTICAL STEPS TO CONSIDER

1. **Train people in your church for prophetic ministry** – It is important to train your people what to do and not do in prophetic ministry so that prophecies will be in line with New Testament models of encouragement, edification, and comfort (1 Corinthians 14:3). Kris Vallotton's *Basic Training For Prophetic Ministry* is a good resource for this.

2. **Give prophetic people an outlet for their words** – As we raise the standard concerning the nature of prophetic words, and as we limit the opportunities of public prophecies for those who do not hold our core values, it is good to give opportunities for prophetically-minded people to influence you as a leader. This sends a message to them that they are valuable. Some of the ways you could do this could be: a) Hold a meeting once every four months or so with prophetic people so they can share what they believe God is showing them. b) Have them email you or a person on your leadership team once a month with what they are hearing. c) Move away from exclusively using spontaneous prophecies in meetings toward a proactive plan of having people communicate with you prior to the service if they have a word.

3. **Equip those who have a heart for worship but who are not on the worship team** – Many churches train flaggers, dancers, artists, and intercessors to join the singers and musicians in creating a powerful worship experience. This training, and the appointing of overall worship leaders, will help funnel people into proper protocols, resulting in healthier relationships.

DECLARATIONS

- I lead a church which is known for the manifest presence of God.
- I have an unusual ability to direct people into healthy outlets for their passions.
- I am not afraid to tell someone "no" about something they feel to do in our services.

SCENARIO

Ronny Revelator pastors Live by the Word Church. He desires to help people hear God personally so they avoid having an unhealthy dependence upon him as the pastor. One person, Paul Hungry, frequently says things like, "God told me to give a prophecy in church today," or "God told me to stay home today," or "God said I should rebuke the congregation for compromising." Pastor Revelator wonders when it is appropriate to say "God said this." If you were Ronny, what would you do?

LIES ASSOCIATED WITH THIS SCENARIO

- People who say "God said" are never wrong.
- People who constantly say "God told me..." are always troublesome people.
- It is unwise to ever challenge anyone who has said, "God said."
- God does not tell individuals things without first clearing it with their leader.

LIFE AND LEADERSHIP CORE VALUES TO CONSIDER

9 I build a culture of feedback in my ministry that I lead by example.
22 I pursue relationship with the strong influencers in places I am called to lead.
28 I regularly educate our people about our ministry's philosophy and process of decision making.
31 Those who regularly influence our ministry are known and trusted.
41 I decrease gossip in our ministry by setting the example of speaking directly with the people that I have a problem with and inviting them to speak directly with me.

DISCERNING WHAT GOD IS DEVELOPING IN ME

- I am learning how to minister effectively to various kinds of people.
- I have the opportunity to grow in my discernment.
- I get to establish life-giving ways for communicating what God is saying.

QUESTIONS TO ASK BEFORE TAKING ACTION

1. What is my philosophy on when it is appropriate to use the "God said" statement?
2. What is this person's track record in hearing from God?
3. How important is it to confront any wrong thinking I may discern in this moment?
4. Am I overreacting to this because of past experiences with such things?
5. Have I equipped the people in my church to hear God's voice and communicate what they heard?

PRACTICAL STEPS TO CONSIDER

1. **Consider replacing the phrase "God told me" with "I believe God told me" as protocol in your ministry** – If we tell others continually, "God told me such and such," it creates a couple problems. First, it makes it difficult for anyone to challenge us if they think we might be wrong – because who wants to argue with God? Second, an overuse of this statement weakens our credibility because it will become clear God did not say everything we attributed to Him. It is better to use "God told me" less frequently and speak, "I believe God told me..." as the norm.

2. **Understand the history of prophetic ministry** – There was a season in church life where most prophetic words seemed to include the phrase, "Thus saith the Lord." These prophecies often happened spontaneously in church meetings when someone felt moved by the Holy Spirit to speak. The use of King James language and strong, "God is saying this" phrases were the norm. This tendency helped create a mindset of needing forceful "God said" language to convince people of what was said (whether it was from God or not). It is the wise person who moves from this mindset and allows their integrity and history of accuracy to be the strength behind the words rather than the overemphasizing of "God said."

3. **Train your people how to effectively communicate what they believe they are hearing from the Lord** – 1 Peter 5:5 says, "God opposes the proud, but gives grace to the humble." It is often prideful to conclude we have the final word on a prophetic message, a doctrinal revelation, or a direction to be taken. As we share what we believe God is giving us in a way that leaves room for the input and influence of others, we create an empowering culture where others feel valued and can bring greater depth to what God is really saying.

DECLARATIONS

- I lead a people who are known to hear clearly from the Lord.
- Our church has a strong, life-giving prophetic ministry.
- I lead a church where people know how to communicate well what they are hearing from God.

SCENARIO

Frank Faith and Perry Presumptuous have a similar philosophy of how to live their Christian life. They believe God has called them to live by faith regarding their immediate needs. They both are talking about quitting their jobs, so they can commit themselves fully to the ministry. They are saying, "God will take care of me." You share concerns about this direction, but they say you are not thinking out of a faith mindset. This puts you in a difficult position. What do you do?

LIES ASSOCIATED WITH THIS SCENARIO

* God prefers that we live from miracle to miracle rather than in an ongoing blessed life.
* God would never ask anyone to quit their job and live by faith.
* Anyone who questions someone who is planning to live by faith is a hindrance and speaking for the devil.
* Having a job is unspiritual and a distraction to God's will for us.

LIFE AND LEADERSHIP CORE VALUES TO CONSIDER

44 I seek to listen and understand before I seek to be heard and understood.
50 I believe people want to do the right thing; therefore, my default belief is to give the benefit of the doubt to others.
19 I have a supernatural personal story as the basis for seemingly risky and illogical things I do.
34 I seek to understand who I am to people and the role I have in their lives.
59 I have a healthy process in decision making.

DISCERNING WHAT GOD IS DEVELOPING IN ME

* I am learning how to understand people better.
* I have the opportunity to develop my own philosophy about what it means to live by faith.
* I get to grow in speaking the truth in love and in how to influence others.

QUESTIONS TO ASK BEFORE TAKING ACTION

1. Who am I to Frank and Perry? What is my role in their lives?
2. What is their track record in hearing the voice of God?
3. What is their "story" from God which causes them to conclude they are to quit their job?
4. How can I equip my people to know the difference between presumption and faith?
5. Is my concern about losing Frank's and/or Perry's financial giving to the church compounding my discernment?

PRACTICAL STEPS TO CONSIDER

1. **Help people understand the difference between faith and presumption –** Big decisions made by faith need to be rooted in a healthy process of decision making which includes: a) being consistent with Scripture, b) a "God story" which indicates divine leading, and c) the involvement of trustworthy people who can attest to the character and to the decision being made. On the contrary, presumptuous decision making is the opposite of these healthy components. It is emotionally driven and tends to want to exercise a one million dollar faith when there has not been a one hundred dollar faith in past experience. Presumption also tends to not want to include others in the decision.

2. **Seek to understand before you seek to be understood –** Whenever possible, take the time to really understand where people are coming from. Learn how to ask good questions: "Can you tell me again your story about why you think you should do this?" "Who have you included in your decision-making process?" As you have a heart to understand, it will increase the likelihood of having true discernment and of having your concerns received.

3. **Be willing to challenge people who need to be challenged –** If you have really heard the person and are not comfortable with a person's faith decision, then share your concerns – "I love your heart to trust God, but I cannot shake the feeling that this direction is not best for you. Could you take more time to pray about this with me?"

DECLARATIONS

- I influence people to live a life of radical faith.
- I have great understanding in knowing the difference between presumption and faith.
- I listen to people and do not jump to conclusions.

SCENARIO

Vinny Vision wants to bring in guest speakers to help move the church forward. As he thinks of the benefits of this, he realizes he does not know the protocols for making this happen. Who should he invite? What should he have them do? How much should he pay them? If you were Pastor Vinny, how would you proceed?

LIES ASSOCIATED WITH THIS SCENARIO

- Guest speakers and special meetings are unimportant for a church.
- I cannot afford to have guest speakers.
- No one would want to come and speak to my ministry.
- If the special speaker is too good, then my people will become dissatisfied with me and wish the special speaker became the pastor.

LIFE AND LEADERSHIP CORE VALUES TO CONSIDER

7   My team and I pursue spiritual fathers and mothers we mutually respect.

73   I intentionally associate with people who are stronger than me in key areas of life and ministry so I will become stronger in those areas.

55   I have an abundance mentality instead of a lack mentality.

26   I err on the side of allowing too much Holy Spirit activity, rather than too little.

8   I pursue "buy-in" from leaders and key people involved before making a big decision.

DISCERNING WHAT GOD IS DEVELOPING IN ME

- I am learning to become more secure in my identity by having people with stronger gifts than me come to influence the ministry.
- I have the opportunity to partner with God to create times of breakthrough for people.
- I get to grow in trusting God to provide everything needed (including finances) to have special speakers.

QUESTIONS TO ASK BEFORE TAKING ACTION

1. Who is the Lord highlighting to me as potential guest speakers for the future?
2. What can I do to make sure the guest speaker has similar core values as I have?
3. What other ministries could I partner with in bringing a speaker to our region?
4. What other leader can I talk with to gain wisdom on hosting guest speakers?
5. Have I cast vision and established buy-in among my team regarding guest speakers?

PRACTICAL STEPS TO CONSIDER

1. **Trust God to highlight the who and the what concerning special speakers –** Guest speakers have the potential to bring great breakthrough in individuals, the ministry, and your geographical area. As you pray and believe God for the specifics, God will start highlighting different ones to you. They could be "big name" speakers, or they could be those who have not traveled much. Either way, you are giving your congregation a great opportunity to receive from God.

2. **Believe and be proactive in securing finances for the special meetings –** Certainly part of this is trusting God, but here are some other ideas to consider: a) Take a special offering at every main meeting for the speaker. b) Designate part of your budget for conferences, guest speakers, and special meetings. c) Partner with other churches (share travel and other expenses). d) Pray in faith over special offerings for speakers, so both the giver and receiver has multiplied blessing.

3. **Understand these basic protocols for having guest speakers –** a) Work with the speaker to agree on a schedule (both for services and non-service times). b) If possible, put them in a hotel or nice home with their own bathroom. c) Communicate your desires for meetings and share any unique things about your culture he/she should be aware of. d) Plan to talk after the first meeting to make sure there are no concerns you or the speaker have. e) Be generous in your honorarium. If you are concerned about the amount you might be able to give, discuss that with speaker prior to his arrival. (Most speakers do not choose to minister based on a certain amount of money, but communication on these matters is important). f) Have him or her meet specifically with your leadership team if at all possible. g) Publicize meetings well.

DECLARATIONS

- I effectively facilitate life-changing special meetings for our ministry with influential speakers.
- I have great wisdom regarding who I should invite to speak at our church.
- The speakers we have at our church feel honored and well taken care of, and they are blessed by our generosity.

"MY LEADER'S SPOUSE DOES NOT ATTEND CHURCH"

SCENARIO

Carl Committed is an elder in Going to the Next Level Church. Pastor Ingrid Ignite is the senior leader. Carl has served well for the last six years. When Carl began as an elder, his wife, Connie, was doing well in her spiritual life and was very committed to the church. In the last two years, she has become increasingly sporadic in attending services and elder social events and is admittedly not doing well in her spiritual life. It has now come to the place where she hardly ever comes at all. If you were Pastor Ignite, what would you do?

LIES ASSOCIATED WITH THIS SCENARIO

- If someone has decided to discontinue coming to church, it means they will never return.
- The quality of a marriage makes no difference to the quality of a ministry.
- If my spouse is struggling spiritually, it means I cannot be in any type of ministry.
- Because this was not addressed earlier, it is now hopeless.

LIFE AND LEADERSHIP CORE VALUES TO CONSIDER

51 I focus more on heart connections than outward obedience toward those I lead.
34 I seek to understand who I am to people and the role i have in their lives.
44 I seek to listen and understand before I seek to be heard and understood.
8   I pursue "buy-in" from leaders and key people involved before making a big decision.
58 I confront people with love and inspire them to grow by reminding them of their destiny.

DISCERNING WHAT GOD IS DEVELOPING IN ME

- I am learning to not just want outward obedience from my leaders but to see the deeper, root issues that need to be addressed in lives and in the overall ministry.
- I have the opportunity to grow in concern for and awareness of the marriages and families of my leaders.
- I get to better develop my philosophy regarding the commitment level of a leader's spouse.

HELP! I'M A PASTOR

QUESTIONS TO ASK BEFORE TAKING ACTION

1. How much is this impacting the health of the church?
2. Is there an individual that Connie trusts that I am in good relationship with?
3. How can I help Carl?
4. Am I okay with having an elder's spouse not attending church?
5. Why has it taken so long to address this situation?

PRACTICAL STEPS TO CONSIDER

1. **Recommit yourself to building people more than building a ministry** – If our ministry is designed to build people, then we are much more likely to discern at an early level problems happening in lives. On the contrary, if we are more vision-focused than people-focused, then there is greater likelihood we (and our leadership team) will miss the signs of trouble in lives. As empowering leaders, we realize our ministry is only as strong as the people leading it; therefore, the health and growth of people is paramount in our minds.

2. **Clarify your standards for leaders** – When I (Steve) pastored my first church, I jokingly said the only requirement for being in leadership is to be a warm body. Although clearly an exaggeration, I did not have the highest standard at first. As we move forward in developing a strong team, it is important that we determine our minimum standards for each level of leadership. Some basic suggestions would be: a) consistent Christian life, b) faithfulness in attendance to ministry, c) faithfulness in tithing and financial giving to the ministry, d) lifestyle of personal and relationship growth, and e) supportive of the senior leader. Regarding the situation we are discussing here, it becomes increasingly important for a spouse of a leader to be a contributing part of the ministry in the higher level leadership positions of the church.

3. **Develop strategies to discern problems in their beginning stages** – A great question is, "When is a problem a problem?" Is it only a problem when the house has burned down, or is it a problem when we see our children playing with matches? Proactive leaders have developed the ability to see problems early on (by seeing them personally or by empowering trusted people to see for them).

DECLARATIONS

- Our ministry is known for having strong marriages and families.
- I have clear and healthy expectations for leaders in our ministry. Our team is in agreement as to what these expectations are.
- I have unusual wisdom and love to minister to the needs of my team.

SCENARIO

Pastor Unita Church is frustrated with the Freedom family who attends her church's special meetings, but does not come on Sunday because they watch Internet services of their favorite revival church. Frank Freedom tells Pastor Church, "We believe God has called us to do church at home as a family. We appreciate what you offer in these special meetings, but we do not believe we are to attend consistently." Unita has noticed that the Freedom family seem to be strong, consistent believers and have children who love God. If you were Pastor Church, would you strongly encourage the Freedoms to start attending a church?

LIES ASSOCIATED WITH THIS SCENARIO

- People who do church in their home are bad people.
- If we disagree with what someone is doing, it means we are dishonoring them.
- Churches who put their services on the Internet are a hindrance to the local church.
- Only a legalistic person would be concerned if someone was not in consistent fellowship.

LIFE AND LEADERSHIP CORE VALUES TO CONSIDER

16   I embrace seasons of building trust in the eyes of those I lead.
38   I pastor a city and region, not just a local church.
35   I adapt my leadership and relational emphasis according to the culture I am in.
61   I have high-level beliefs about the people I lead and desire to influence.
70   I am more for things than I am against things.

DISCERNING WHAT GOD IS DEVELOPING IN ME

- I am learning how to become an increased strength to all believers in my region.
- I have the opportunity to evaluate how my church can grow in reaching different kinds of people.
- I get to celebrate believers in my area who have a great hunger for God.

HELP! I'M A PASTOR

QUESTIONS TO ASK BEFORE TAKING ACTION

1. Am I more concerned about building my church than what God is doing in people?
2. How can I be a blessing to this family?
3. How can we become stronger in reaching those who have become disillusioned by church?
4. How can we increase a value for being connected with a local group of people?
5. Should I share my concerns with this family? If so, how and when?

PRACTICAL STEPS TO CONSIDER

1. **Understand why many Christians do not attend traditional churches** – It is too simplistic to say people who do not attend a church regularly are out of God's will. Some do not come because they have had very negative experiences in church. Others do not have a revelation of the importance of consistent fellowship. There are also those who have challenging family dynamics which affect the ability to make a church commitment. Certainly some are distracted by wrong priorities and undisciplined living. Whatever the reason, it is always good to understand people before labeling them as wrong or uncommitted.

2. **Determine to "pastor" a region, not just your church** – It is small thinking to only consider yourself the shepherd of the people who attend your ministry. Something powerful happens when we take spiritual ownership of a city or region. The success of our ministry is not determined by how many people attend on a weekend, but it is to be judged by the influence we have on the widest spectrum of people – including other churches and those who do church at home. This positive impact will increase exponentially when we do it out of pure motives, and not out of selfish ambition.

3. **Articulate life-giving beliefs about the importance of being in consistent fellowship** – Many leaders have used Hebrews 10:25 as a spiritual club in an attempt to knock sense into inconsistent church attendees ("not forsaking the assembling together as is the manner of some"), but using Scripture as a law probably will not help most people. Great leaders have the ability to inspire people to do what they formerly did not want to do.

DECLARATIONS

- I love Christians who do church at their home and am a blessing to them.
- Because of the amount of life in our church, people can hardly stay away.
- I am able to articulate great beliefs about why Christians should commit to consistent fellowship.

SCENARIO

Pastor Chris Charisma is the good-looking dynamic pastor of Going Forward Church. He is married to Carla. They have three children who are still living at home. The Charisma's marriage is struggling some, and Carla is not as interested in sex anymore. Chris is frustrated and is noticing a young divorcée in his leadership team, Gina Perfect, in a way he has not before. She regularly tells Chris what a great leader he is and has been flirting with him on a consistent basis. Chris is tempted to pursue Gina. If you were Pastor Chris, what would you do?

LIES ASSOCIATED WITH THIS SCENARIO

- It is impossible to affair-proof a church.
- Only very uncommitted Christians would ever be tempted to have an affair.
- Our ministry is not effective in helping people who are tempted to have an affair or who have had one.
- It is absolutely impossible for an affair to ever happen in my family or in the lives of those I do ministry with.

LIFE AND LEADERSHIP CORE VALUES TO CONSIDER

54 I have high standards in how I conduct myself in relationships with the opposite sex.

57 I purpose to have my family respect me more than the people I lead respect me.

49 I am "sent" by trustworthy people into the ministry I have, and I continue to pursue accountability with them.

74 I have at least one person in my life with whom I share the deep things of my life with (things such as disappointments, weaknesses, dreams, fears, and longings).

75 I prioritize my emotional well-being.

DISCERNING WHAT GOD IS DEVELOPING IN ME

- I am learning to set good boundaries in my actions and thoughts.
- I have the opportunity to prioritize my marriage above every other human relationship.
- I get to have my deepest needs met by God, not by people.

QUESTIONS TO ASK BEFORE TAKING ACTION

1. How can I make my marriage a priority over ministry?
2. How can I send stronger signals that I am unavailable for an affair?
3. What safeguards does our ministry have (and what can we establish) to decrease the likelihood of affairs?
4. When will I open up to share my battle with my spouse and/or another person?
5. What is the root problem I am battling?

PRACTICAL STEPS TO CONSIDER

Note: We are referring to a male tempted to have an affair, but the principles can be applied to women as well.

1. **Establish standards to help "affair proof" your life and church** – Here are some ideas: a) Never meet alone with another woman beside your wife. b) Do not get into intimate conversations with other women. c) Never discuss the weaknesses of your wife with another woman. d) Regularly share "I love my wife" messages. e) Keep investing in your own marriage. f) Pursue more information on how to "affair-proof" your marriage. There is a lot of good information available.

2. **Understand the devastation affairs cause** – The common results of pastors and leaders having an affair include broken trust in marriage, divorce, individuals becoming disillusioned with the church and Christianity, damaged reputations, alimony and child support payments, wayward and distant children, and more. In contrast, get a vision for the joy of living out a righteous relationship.

3. **Lead a ministry that addresses the emotional wounds of people** – It is wise and loving for a leader to take steps to insure the members of his or her leadership team really are healthy. This can be done in many ways. One way is through having inner healing and biblically based counseling ministries pour into the leaders and congregation to strengthen them and help heal the wounds of negative experiences. (These can also help those who might have already had an affair.) As our people become emotionally healthy, they are less likely to have affairs.

DECLARATIONS

- The ministry I lead has healthy marriages and great protection against affairs.
- My leaders and I have a plan to insure we are growing in emotional health.
- The influencers in our ministry have powerful, life-giving strategies that dramatically decrease the likelihood of affairs in our lives and ministries.

SCENARIO

Perry and Pam Passion lead The Church of the Committed. They seemingly have a normal schedule of church events. Lately, Pastor Passion has noticed key leaders resistant to any new ideas or direction. Leaders like Mack Minister and Elsie Elder just do not want to do anything new or out of the normal routine (e.g. special services, leadership retreats, etc.). Mack and Elsie frequently say they and the other leaders are tired. This frustrates the Passions. If you were the Passions, what would you do?

LIES ASSOCIATED WITH THIS SCENARIO

- The people who are not excited about what I propose are always the problem; it is never me.
- Tired people have never done anything significant.
- If leaders are tired, it automatically means we should do less things in church.
- The best answer for people who constantly say they are tired is "Quit your bellyaching and get over it!"

LIFE AND LEADERSHIP CORE VALUES TO CONSIDER

51 I focus more on heart connections than outward obedience toward those I lead.

14 I am more concerned about building people than I am concerned about building a ministry.

6 I lead a culture of radical encouragement.

30 I tell those I lead who they are much more than I tell them what to do.

8 I pursue "buy-in" from leaders and key people involved before making a big decision.

DISCERNING WHAT GOD IS DEVELOPING IN ME

- I am learning to focus on the overall health of each of my leaders.
- I have the opportunity to evaluate and communicate the commitment level needed by those on my leadership team.
- I get to inspire my leaders at a higher level.

QUESTIONS TO ASK BEFORE TAKING ACTION

1. Have I talked personally with Mack and Elsie to find out what the root issue is and if health, personal, or family problems are draining them of energy?

2. What can I do to increase the core team in the next year or two?

3. What deeper thing might my leaders be trying to say to me about a problem they see in my leadership?

4. How can I involve my team members more in the event-planning process?

PRACTICAL STEPS TO CONSIDER

1. **Increase the amount of encouragement on your leadership team and in the church** – Tiredness in a ministry is often the result of a lack of encouragement. Ideas to overcome this are: a) Make it a goal that each team member encourage at least one person at every meeting possible through specific thanksgiving. b) Put someone in the "hot seat" to receive prophetic words from the others at leadership meetings. c) Designate someone as "Encouragement and Gratitude Facilitator" who will help the ministry be radically encouraging and thankful. Great leaders inspire people. Inspired people are less tired and have more vision. The more vision one has for their future, the more power and energy they have for the present.

2. **Recommit to building people as a greater priority than building a ministry** – The strength of a ministry is dependent upon the strength of its leaders. One of the senior leader's main callings is to raise up and nurture other leaders. This involves building heart connections, growing together, and being quick to be aware of how people are really doing.

3. **Live a life of love that inspires others to a lifestyle of sacrificial leadership** – Yes, we are to be sensitive to not overwork our core team, but it needs to be understood that leadership is part of the "greater love" of laying down our lives for others (John 15:13). "He who is greatest among you shall be your servant" (Matthew 23:11). God has called us to love and serve with our time and money, through difficulty and through tiredness. Great leaders model commitment and are not afraid to call their people to do so the same.

DECLARATIONS

- I never leave a meeting without giving someone a word of encouragement.
- Our leaders live sacrificially for the kingdom and inspire others to do the same.
- I intuitively help my leadership team manage their lives successfully.

SCENARIO

Rich N. Love is senior pastor of The Happy Church. It is a church of 250 people with four pastors on staff, including Associate Pastor Sam Climite. Pastor Love has been leading the church for three years, and Sam was there when he came. Sam is very pastoral but struggles to complete goals and to follow through on Rich's requests of him. Whenever Pastor Love speaks to Sam about these things, Sam becomes defensive. He has accused Rich of being controlling and nit-picking. Rich sees this situation as blockage to growth and to the overall leadership development in the church. He believes Sam needs to be let go from his position. If you were Pastor Rich, what would you do?

LIES ASSOCIATED WITH THIS SCENARIO

- It is not honoring or loving to remove someone from a leadership position.
- If a leader on our church staff is not performing well, they should be fired immediately.
- The most important goals in pastoring a church is to have everyone like me.
- It does not take courage to lead a church.

LIFE AND LEADERSHIP CORE VALUES TO CONSIDER

44 I seek to listen and understand before I seek to be heard and understood.

7 My team and I pursue spiritual fathers and mothers we mutually respect.

65 I recognize that trust for one another in our leadership team is a necessary ingredient for our ministry to go forward.

9 I build a culture of feedback in my ministry that I lead by example.

58 I confront people with love and inspire them to grow by reminding them of their destiny.

DISCERNING WHAT GOD IS DEVELOPING IN ME

- I am learning to keep a strong love for people amidst difficult relationship situations.
- I have the opportunity to discern God's timing in making changes on my team.
- I get to establish higher standards of leadership.

QUESTIONS TO ASK BEFORE TAKING ACTION

1. Is any bitterness in my own heart complicating how I am seeing this person and situation?
2. How will the church be impacted if he is removed from leadership now?
3. Who do Sam and I mutually respect who can help in the situation?
4. Am I accountable to others in how I am conducting my relationship with Sam?
5. What role do the other leaders in the church have regarding this? How can these leaders and I work together in the most healthy way?

PRACTICAL STEPS TO CONSIDER

1. **Clarify the real issues** – When there is disagreement between the senior leader and a staff member (or a key volunteer leader), one of the most important issues to be addressed is the lack of trust in the relationship. "This cannot work long term if the broken trust between us is not restored. What can I do for you to trust me more? Here is what I need for me to start trusting you at a higher level."

2. **Identify who can help you** – It is usually unwise to try to resolve ongoing conflict by yourself. Matthew 18:15-17 gives a pattern of having an unbiased and respected person help in this process. The senior leader also would be prudent (if it is possible) to include both of the other leaders in the church and the mothers/fathers of the ministry not in the city to help in the situation. Finally, the senior leader needs feedback on how he or she is leading the church and concerning the standards for leadership he or she has.

3. **Consider these steps in removing an underperforming leader or staff member if they are not in agreement with leaving** – a) Work to find other opportunities for them. b) Consult your Constitution and By-laws (if it does not specifically address what to do in situations like this, upgrade this document after this incident is over). c) Seek out wisdom from experienced leaders (and your attorney). d) If this person is on staff, give them a generous severance package. e) Avoid slandering this leader. f) Do not be in a hurry unless serious damage is happening to the church. g) Use great wisdom in the wording of what is shared with the congregation.

DECLARATIONS

- I have great love and wisdom in helping leaders who are struggling to fulfill their ministry duties.
- My life and ministry constantly attracts and produces strong leaders.
- Our ministry is protected from division, and growing in unity and trust.

SCENARIO

Phil U. Moore is the senior pastor of New Wine Church, a church of 150. It Is not unusual for people to "manifest" in church meetings. During this particular season in church life, the manifestations are increasing on Sunday mornings. One person, Lucy Fireball, regularly erupts in loud laughter and cannot seem to control it. It is especially common when she sits by Sally Ignite. Visitors have walked out because of Lucy. If you were Pastor Moore, what would you do?

LIES ASSOCIATED WITH THIS SCENARIO

- If I confront Lucy and Sally, I am quenching the Holy Spirit.
- One of my main goals as a pastor is to make sure there is never anything unusual or uncomfortable happening in our ministry.
- Freedom in our meetings means that everyone can do whatever they feel like doing, and if I try to limit certain things from happening, I am a controlling leader.
- If good people are leaving church meetings, the manifestations cannot be from God.

LIFE AND LEADERSHIP CORE VALUES TO CONSIDER

26 I err on the side of allowing too much Holy Spirit activity, rather than too little.
22 I pursue relationships with the strong influencers in places I am called to lead.
28 I regularly educate our people about our ministry's philosophy and process of decision making.
53 I help people understand how their behavior impacts others.
58 I confront people with love and inspire them to grow by reminding them of their destiny.

DISCERNING WHAT GOD IS DEVELOPING IN ME

- I am learning how to strengthen the way I lead regarding the moving of the Holy Spirit.
- I have the opportunity to understand the hearts of people before making a major conclusion or decision.
- I get to lead a ministry that is free of unnecessary distractions.

QUESTIONS TO ASK BEFORE TAKING ACTION

1. What has God called our ministry to emphasize?
2. Am I being reactive or proactive in this decision?
3. Do I have the support of my leadership team in the direction I am going?
4. Am I willing to bless people in leaving the church for this reason?
5. Am I willing to confront people in my ministry who are unnecessarily distracting?

PRACTICAL STEPS TO CONSIDER

1. **Clarify your philosophy on the "move of the Holy Spirit"** – It is important to proactively establish and articulate the protocols about what behaviors are deemed as "out of order." Certainly God has been known to bypass man's guidelines for meetings (ha ha), but the wise senior and core leaders will proactively share their philosophy on these things to the church.

2. **Value the "Holy Spirit" people of your ministry** – It is a mistake for the senior leader to ignore or not connect with those who are avidly pursuing more of the Spirit in their lives (even though they at times can be a little unpredictable). If the pastor does not feel he or she connects well with them, then he or she should have a trusted leader in the church help "oversee" this catalytic group.

3. **Develop a plan to increase "God encounters" and reduce unnecessary distractions in your ministry** – To increase God encounters: a) Pursue Holy Spirit as a leadership team. b) Have guest speakers emphasize the value and importance of Holy Spirit. c) Regularly share testimonies about this. d) Preach through the Book of Acts. e) Start and participate in regular Holy Spirit meetings at church. To decrease unnecessary "Holy Spirit" distractions: a) Pursue relationship with those who are distracting services, hear their story, and help them see the bigger picture. b) Teach the principles of 1 Corinthians 14 about group edification vs. individuals doing their own thing. c) Give "Holy Spirit outlets" for people outside of regular meetings. d) Enlist loving but persuasive people to communicate with and redirect those who are causing unnecessary distractions in meetings. e) Err on the side of letting too much happen (consider Uzzah in 2 Samuel 6:6).

DECLARATIONS

- People dramatically encounter God in ministries I lead.
- I have great wisdom in balancing the move of the Spirit and creating an environment where people feel safe and protected.
- I am building stronger heart connections with influencers in our environment.

SCENARIO

Pastor Excel Lent is disappointed again. He has planned special meetings for months with guest speaker, Andy Anointed. He feels he has promoted the meetings well, but he is battling the familiar spirit of foreboding again – the fear that few people would come to the meetings. As Pastor Excel stands up to open the first meeting, he is inwardly defeated by the low attendance. He notices people not there – specifically two of his elders, Ingrid Influential and Larry Leaders. More names come to his mind. As Pastor Lent opens the meeting, he cannot stop thinking, "Important people are always missing our special services." If you were Pastor Lent, what would you do?

LIES ASSOCIATED WITH THIS SCENARIO

- If the people of the church really loved me as their pastor, they would always be at the special services I plan.
- It would be legalistic and controlling to ask my leaders to come to the church's special meetings.
- I need to make those who did not come to the special meetings feel guilty so they will come in the future.
- A meeting cannot be powerful if everyone is not there, so I should stop having special meetings.

LIFE AND LEADERSHIP CORE VALUES TO CONSIDER

8   I pursue "buy-in" from leaders and key people involved before making a big decision.
50 I believe people want to do the right thing; therefore, my default belief is to give the benefit of the doubt to others.
52 I am a God-pleaser, not a people-pleaser.
66 I motivate people through vision instead of guilt and manipulation.
48 My response to something is almost always more important than the something.

DISCERNING WHAT GOD IS DEVELOPING IN ME

- I am learning to dwell on what God is doing rather than what I perceive to not be happening.
- I have the opportunity to walk in faith about decisions I have made.
- I get to keep my beliefs strong about those who are disappointing me.

QUESTIONS TO ASK BEFORE TAKING ACTION

1. Why does this bother me so much?
2. How much buy-in do I have from other leaders before I plan special meetings?
3. Do my people sense that I understand their commitments outside of church?
4. Have my leaders and I agreed about their level of commitment to the church?
5. Are there important people in my ministry for whom it is unrealistic to come to special meetings?

PRACTICAL STEPS TO CONSIDER

1. **See your disappointment as a bigger problem than people not attending the meetings** – Unresolved disappointment is like a cancer in the life of a leader. It leads to blame-shifting, victim mentalities, law-driven motivational techniques, decreased heart connections with people, and missing out on seeing the good things that are actually happening. Every great leader has had to learn how to not be neutralized or deadened by disappointing circumstances. Our response to something is almost always more important than the "something."

2. **Choose to focus more on what is happening rather than what seems to not be happening** – A leader with vision will stir up enthusiasm for what is happening. This leader will say things like, "There are people here! God does not need many people for something big to happen! This meeting could be catalytic to worldwide transformation! Those not here are great people, and God is going to bless them radically with the overflow of these meetings! God is going to change my life tonight! There will be a mighty deposit left in the spirit realm tonight which will affect this region for decades to come!"

3. **Get a plan to develop greater buy-in from your leaders and people for special meetings** – a) Work with your leaders to develop the overall philosophy of the purpose and frequency of meetings in your ministry. b) Use a master calendar to coordinate the timing of key church events. c) Find ways for leaders and others in your church to be activated during special meetings. d) Have the guest speaker meet with leaders while he or she is at the church. e) Build and inspire vision in the church through your messages and in other ways about special meetings.

DECLARATIONS

- We have powerful services no matter how many are in attendance.
- Our leaders and people have great buy-in to the extra meetings we have planned to equip the church and bring breakthrough.
- I am healed from disappointment and celebrate regularly what God is doing.

SCENARIO

Pastor Phil Phaithful is wondering if it is time to leave Rock Church. He has been the senior leader for six years. He came at a time of difficulty in the church and has brought stability and growth. He wonders if another leadership style would take them into their next season, or if he needs to try to adapt his leadership style to the current needs of the church. He is 55 and his financial situation is creating some fear in him as he considers leaving. If you were Pastor Phil, what would you do?

LIES ASSOCIATED WITH THIS SCENARIO

- God is frustrated with me, so He does not want to talk with me.
- I am a person with limited options in life.
- My financial provision depends on this church.
- No long-term pastor of a church has ever felt like he or she was done serving there.

LIFE AND LEADERSHIP CORE VALUES TO CONSIDER

2   I strongly prioritize and protect my "secret place" times with the Lord.
7   My team and I pursue spiritual fathers and mothers we mutually respect.
17 I thrive in uncertainty, difficulty, and unresolved situations because I have a "word" from the Lord.
42 I am primarily a developer of leaders.
59 I have a healthy process in decision making.

DISCERNING WHAT GOD IS DEVELOPING IN ME

- I am learning to trust in Him regarding my future.
- I have the opportunity to discover what my church needs in its next season.
- I get to prepare for the next season of my life wherever it might be.

QUESTIONS TO ASK BEFORE TAKING ACTION

1. What indicators are influencing my decision to leave or stay?
2. Who can I talk with to help me discern what God is doing in the church and in me?
3. What might I be running from, and what am I moving toward?
4. What does the church need to go into its next season? Do I have the passion, vision, and/or strategies to take it there?
5. What can I do to increase the likelihood of knowing what to do?

PRACTICAL STEPS TO CONSIDER

1. **Clarify what God has said and is saying** – Here are tips to help you do that: a) Spend extra time in the secret place. Get away for a time to be refreshed and to see from a higher perspective. b) Revisit what God has told you in the past. Review the promises and prophetic words over your life. c) Put yourself in environments where God can speak to you personally and through prophetic people. Note unusual coincidences. d) Talk with people you trust and who know you well. e) Make two lists – one with indicators for staying and one with indicators for leaving. Thank God repeatedly that you will know what to do.

2. **Move forward in your life** – "And the Lord said to Moses, 'Why do you cry to Me? Tell the children of Israel to go forward.'" (Exodus 14:15). God basically told the hemmed in Israelites, "Stop begging me to do something and move forward in your lives." As they did, the Red Sea parted. Indeed one of the best questions we can ask is, "What does it mean for me to move forward in my life?" Something powerful happens when we move forward in personal growth, change, learning, stretching, risking, and improving. Too often in times of double-mindedness we become neutralized and quit progressing. This will only compound our inner struggles.

3. **Position yourself and the church for the next season** – A good church leader model is for the senior leaders to be constantly trying "to work themselves out of a job" – to focus on raising people up who can lead, preach, and administrate the things of the ministry. Senior leaders do not want the church to have an unhealthy dependence on any one leader. It is also generally wise for the pastor to prepare for the future by having other streams of income coming into the family besides the church salary. This will make future decisions of staying or leaving less encumbered by financial considerations.

DECLARATIONS

- God loves me and will take care of me in incredible ways.
- I will always know what to do.
- This next season is going to be the best season for the church and for my life.

SCENARIO

Pastor Ernie M. Powerment has developed a team of leaders to help him lead and to share in the preaching ministry. Recently Ronny Revelator shared a message based on a book he is reading entitled, *Annihilating Sacred Cows in the Church.* Ernie thinks some of what Ronny said was unscriptural. While Ernie believes we will continually see new things in Scripture to be taught, he now realizes some of those who teach and preach have never had any formal Bible or theological training. He is concerned about this and the potential for heresy. If you were Ernie, what would you do?

LIES ASSOCIATED WITH THIS SCENARIO

* As long as a person has a good heart and has "been with Jesus," we should not question what he or she preaches.
* If someone is accused of teaching heresy, it is always true.
* Pastors who would have concerns about new revelations must be controlling and have a religious spirit.
* All truth from the Bible has already been revealed, so we should always be suspicious of anything preached that we have not heard before.

LIFE AND LEADERSHIP CORE VALUES TO CONSIDER

5   I equip people with the basic principles of how to interpret the Bible.
3   I build "bridges" in my teachings to help people move into the deeper things of God.
58   I confront people with love and inspire them to grow by reminding them of their destiny.
51   I focus more on heart connections than outward obedience toward those I lead.
65   I recognize that trust for one another in our leadership team is a necessary ingredient for our ministry to go forward.

DISCERNING WHAT GOD IS DEVELOPING IN ME

* I am learning to be vigilant in establishing my ministry as a safe place.
* I have the opportunity to develop good accountability in what we teach as a leadership team.
* I get to become stronger in my biblical doctrine while still being open to fresh perspectives on Scripture.

QUESTIONS TO ASK BEFORE TAKING ACTION

1. What protocols keep us accountable for what we teach and preach?
2. Do I really understand what Ronny is trying to say?
3. Is this a one time thing or a pattern for Ronny?
4. Is my goal to discover truth or seek agreement on my current understanding?
5. Is this really heresy, or am I stuck in a wrong belief?

PRACTICAL STEPS TO CONSIDER

1. **Regularly train teachers and preachers** – One of the main responsibilities of senior leaders is to equip their people to become leaders. Part of this equipping will include training in how to teach and preach. These "preaching classes" give opportunities for people to grow in their overall skill and anointing in sharing God's word. Protocols for proper biblical interpretation should be part of these classes. It is recommended that everyone who preaches and teaches in the church be a part of an annual refresher class including these protocols.

2. **Teach your people how to properly interpret the Bible** – One of the greatest privileges of pastoral leadership is to help people connect personally to God. One main aspect of this assignment is to inspire a love for the Bible and to release strategies for its proper interpretation.

3. **Go after greater revelation but establish safety measures to lessen the chances of wrong doctrine being taught** – Some examples of good safety measures are: a) In order to discuss new revelations being received, develop a group of people to meet with regularly who are hungry for God, believe in the present day power of the Holy Spirit, and who honor the authority of Scripture. b) Take time to live out major doctrinal shifts before dogmatically teaching them. c) When finally sharing these truths, immerse your sermons in Scripture and insert the phrase, "This is what I am not saying..." to avoid misunderstandings in what you are revealing. One final thought – every new revelation from God has been called heretical by someone, so do not be afraid of pursuing fresh understanding from the Bible.

DECLARATIONS

- Our church loves the Bible and has increasing revelation of it.
- Our preachers and teachers have a strong revelatory and biblical foundation for what is taught.
- The five fold office of teacher releases supernatural life in our midst and helps us test what it is being revealed to us.

SCENARIO

Pastor Perry Pleaser from Friendly Church probably has too high of a value for having people like him and appreciate what he does. He actually is mystified why someone as good-hearted as him could have people who seem to not like him. Perry is currently struggling inwardly about one person in his church, Res Erved, a successful businessman who is a big financial giver into Friendly Church. Res is not excited about the direction Perry is leading the church. Perry feels tongue-tied and intimidated around Res. Pastor Pleaser also finds himself dwelling on Res during his messages and free time. If you were Pastor Pleaser, what would you do?

LIES ASSOCIATED WITH THIS SCENARIO

- Anyone who is not excited about my leadership is clearly in partnership with the devil.
- If I have strong feelings of intimidation now, it means I always will.
- No successful pastor has ever felt intimidated by anyone in his or her church.
- My goal as a pastor is to make sure everyone in the church agrees with me.

LIFE AND LEADERSHIP CORE VALUES TO CONSIDER

52 I am a God-pleaser, not a people-pleaser.
44 I seek to listen and understand before I seek to be heard and understood.
61 I have high-level beliefs about the people I lead and desire to influence.
16 I embrace seasons of building trust in the eyes of those I lead.
73 I intentionally associate with people who are stronger than me in key areas of life and ministry so I will become stronger in those areas.

DISCERNING WHAT GOD IS DEVELOPING IN ME

- I am learning to thrive even if not everyone celebrates me.
- I have the opportunity to grow as a person and a leader.
- I get to overcome any tendency of being a people-pleaser rather than a God-pleaser.

QUESTIONS TO ASK BEFORE TAKING ACTION

1. What is the root lie which causes me to dwell on the people who are not celebrating me or my decisions?
2. Why is it so important to me for everyone to be happy with my leadership?
3. Who on my team has a good relationship with Res? How could they help?
4. How can I build greater trust in the eyes of people like Res?
5. What lies might create an unhealthy concern in me about losing people like Res from the ministry?

PRACTICAL STEPS TO CONSIDER

1. **Pursue healthy "identity beliefs" for greater confidence in your life and leadership** – One of the most life-changing revelations is to hear and believe who God says we are rather than believing who our past experience says we are. Many of the attributes we call our personality are simply bad beliefs, and these beliefs can be changed. Feelings of intimidation and insecurity are a wakeup call to replace lies with truth about our identity; and as we embrace truth, we will be made free (confident) in our lives and in our relationships.

2. **Build trust in the eyes of those you lead but do not depend on them as your source** – It should not surprise us that some people need time before they trust leaders. Instead of trying to please people, it would be better to behave in ways that build trust (e.g. consistency, follow-through, personal growth, love, authenticity, etc.). As we focus more on these, instead of making people happy so they will support us, we will build respect in the eyes of others and usually overcome initial hesitations about our leadership and about us.

3. **Have a big vision which attracts big people** – We are not going to attract or keep every major influencer we meet, but if we keep advancing in life, in vision to change the world, and in courage, we will increasingly draw to us people who are "big" on the inside. These influencers will gather to us because they want to help us, and they believe being with us is catalytic for them. Instead of dwelling on those who are not on board with what we are doing, realize if we keep our focus on moving forward, we will not lack quality people around us.

DECLARATIONS

*   I do not have a spirit of fear, but a spirit of power, love and a sound mind.
*   People determine I am a trustworthy leader who they want to partner with.
*   I stay strong in inner victory and purpose when people are not supportive of me.

SCENARIO

Senior Pastor Cynthia Sincere of Peace Ministries does not know if she can take another phone call or read another email about what is happening in the lives of her leaders and church attendees. Yesterday, she got a call from the wife of an elder saying she is leaving her husband. The day before, the men's ministries leader admitted to a serious pornography problem. Today, she heard two people in the church are suing each other because of a business deal that went bad. Cynthia tells her husband, "Everyone's lives seem to be falling apart in our church! What is happening?" If you were Cynthia, what would you do?

LIES ASSOCIATED WITH THIS SCENARIO

- If I am sincere, I will never experience any difficulties in life.
- Churches making a difference should expect constant negative spiritual attacks on its leaders and people.
- There is nothing we can do to decrease the amount of troubles the people of our church face.
- Pastors who have a series of difficult circumstances in the church should just quit.

LIFE AND LEADERSHIP CORE VALUES TO CONSIDER

1   There is always a solution for every situation I face.
10   I create opportunities for those in my church to encounter God in powerful ways.
17   I thrive in uncertainty, difficulty, and unresolved situations because I have a "word" from the Lord.
74   I have at least one person in my life with whom I share the deep things of my life with (things such as disappointments, weaknesses, dreams, fears, and longings).
60   God works all things together for good in my ministry.

DISCERNING WHAT GOD IS DEVELOPING IN ME

- I am learning how to release hope in the most difficult circumstances.
- I have the opportunity to draw near to the Lord for His strength.
- I get to feel the pains of people and to "weep with those who weep."

HELP! I'M A PASTOR

QUESTIONS TO ASK BEFORE TAKING ACTION

1. How can we strengthen the intercession of our ministry?
2. Is the Holy Spirit showing me any spiritual roots for what is happening?
3. Does our ministry focus more on the devil's attacks or God's protection?
4. What steps can we take to increase our ministry to those who are hurting and going through difficulty?
5. What am I supposed to do to help those in crisis? What am I not supposed to do?

PRACTICAL STEPS TO CONSIDER

1. **Realize that long-standing issues seem to surface in a grace and empowerment culture** – Is it possible that issues do not actually come to the light until people are in environments where they will be loved and restored? Could it be ministries with wisdom, love, and the power of God attract people who are ready for their deep breakthrough? If this is true, then having people in our church struggling is often a compliment to us, not an indication that something is wrong.

2. **Revisit your beliefs about blessing, suffering, mystery, and protection** – There are two opposing theological beliefs which complicate the leading of our ministries through challenging times. The first is an overemphasis on Satanic attacks – with the subtle, problem-causing belief that spiritual people will always be under attack. The other is the belief those close to Jesus will not face challenges in life – which often disconnects us with the pain people are experiencing. It is best to believe that as the kingdom advances there will be less curses and more blessings in our midst. As we battle with crisis in our ministry, we trust God to meet the need before us, but we also remain relentless to see our ministry live in the abundant life Jesus bought for us (including the blessing and protection of the Lord).

3. **Take care of yourself** – Have people pray for you and your church. Do not feel you have to be the answer for everyone's needs, but equip and activate people to be a strength for others. Realize some issues have been in existence for a long time, and it does not require an emergency response from you. Remember, the phrase "It came to pass," and be glad it does not say, "It came to stay."

DECLARATIONS

- We have a powerful ministry of restoration.
- We love people through pain and difficulty.
- Our ministry increasingly sees people walk in blessing and protection.

SCENARIO

Louise Love is the new pastor at Rich Relationships Ministries. She has never performed a wedding ceremony, but in a short span of time she has had three couples ask her if she would officiate their weddings. The first to ask are two teenagers from the youth group who are expecting a child together. The next is a young man and woman who just came back from two years of ministry school. The third couple is a man and woman who have both been divorced. The woman attends Pastor Love's church, but the man does not (and it is unclear if the man is even saved). Pastor Love wonders if she should perform all these ceremonies. If you were her, what would you do?

LIES ASSOCIATED WITH THIS SCENARIO

- I should marry every couple who asks me to do so.
- Performing wedding ceremonies is an unimportant part of pastoral ministry.
- Couples who are really in love do not need premarital counseling.
- I should never involve myself in the lives of people who are not close to God because it could ruin my reputation.

LIFE AND LEADERSHIP CORE VALUES TO CONSIDER

77 My ministry provides regular training and education on key life skills.
38 I pastor a city and region, not just a local church.
28 I regularly educate our people about our ministry's philosophy and process of decision making.
19 I have a supernatural personal story as the basis for seemingly risky and illogical things I do.
52 I am a God-pleaser, not a people-pleaser.

DISCERNING WHAT GOD IS DEVELOPING IN ME

- I am learning how to have high standards without being unloving or legalistic.
- I have the opportunity to increase my ministry's influence on families and marriages.
- I get to be proactive in developing and communicating my philosophy concerning performing weddings.

QUESTIONS TO ASK BEFORE TAKING ACTION

1. What other pastors can I talk with to help me?
2. What legal requirements are there for those performing wedding ceremonies?
3. What values are important to our church leadership team that I should consider?
4. Have I determined my theological beliefs related to divorce and remarriage, doing weddings for non-Christians, etc.?
5. How can I leverage the skill of our team members who have a heart for marriages?

PRACTICAL STEPS TO CONSIDER

1. **Develop your philosophy and standards for who you will perform weddings for** – When a couple asks you to marry them, do not say yes right away unless you know them very well. Have them fill out a premarital questionnaire prior to the first meeting to understand their history, compatibility, spirituality, etc. In the first meeting say something like, "I need to be comfortable that you are ready for marriage before I agree to do the ceremony." Also, it is important to clarify your beliefs about marrying couples when there is divorce, pregnancy, a non-Christian, etc. It is good to discuss these types of things with seasoned ministers you trust to glean from their thoughts and experience.

2. **Develop a strong premarital counseling and training plan** – It is generally recommended pastors do not do a wedding ceremony in which there has not been premarital counseling. This counseling should be the confirmation in the process for the decision to get married, but this goal is often short-circuited because many couples are far along in the process before seeing you. You can proactively prepare for this tendency by having your wedding protocols in a packet or online for the couple to review before the first meeting and by sharing your beliefs regularly with your congregation about these things to develop a culture regarding the purpose of engagement and the wedding.

3. **Develop a team of people from your ministry to pour into marriages and families** – Raise up a couple or couples who can become your designated marriage coaches. They would oversee (or help oversee with you) the church's ministry to married couples and those desiring to be married.

DECLARATIONS

- Our ministry creates strong marriages.
- I have great wisdom in deciding what couples I will perform a ceremony for.
- We have an incredible team pouring into married couples and people desiring to get married.

SCENARIO

Pastor Ernie Efficient keeps hearing his people say, "We would love to participate in that, but we are so busy, and we don't have time right now." He feels like there is an epidemic of people saying they are in a very busy season of life. Ernie almost blew a gasket when he heard Igor Influential say, "We have too many meetings in this church. Don't you know we have busy lives?" If you were Pastor Efficient, what would you do?

LIES ASSOCIATED WITH THIS SCENARIO

- People who say they are too busy to participate in our church programs are uncommitted, lukewarm Christians.
- Teaching on time management is an unspiritual emphasis for a pastor.
- I should make a business person in my church feel guilty if he or she cannot attend as many meetings as someone who is retired.
- It would be insensitive to call people to a high-level commitment to our church and its ministries.

LIFE AND LEADERSHIP CORE VALUES TO CONSIDER

68 I have a strong ability to make people feel needed, valued, and loved in our ministry as opposed to them feeling used.
61 I have high-level beliefs about the people I lead and desire to influence.
77 My ministry provides regular training and education on key life skills.
33 I measure success by how many of our people are advancing the kingdom outside of the church walls.
35 I adapt my leadership and relational emphasis according to the culture I am in.

DISCERNING WHAT GOD IS DEVELOPING IN ME

- I am learning how to insure that all events in my ministry are vital.
- I have the opportunity to understand the culture of the people I am called to reach.
- I get to inspire and equip busy people to effectively manage their schedules.

QUESTIONS TO ASK BEFORE TAKING ACTION

1. Do my people perceive that I understand what their lives are really like?

2. What can I do to help my people believe I value their time, but still call them to a high commitment in our ministry?

3. Who in our ministry has an anointing to help our leaders and church attendees manage their time and lives in a healthy manner?

4. Do I give the impression that the only way to be truly committed is by being faithful at all our church meetings?

5. What can I do to grow in my personal time management?

PRACTICAL STEPS TO CONSIDER

1. **Increase your ability to motivate people in a life-giving way** – It is difficult to inspire and motivate others if we are frustrated, disappointed, angry, too focused on rules, or have lost our belief in the people we are leading. We can motivate people if we: a) demonstrate we are more concerned about them than our ministry, b) equip them with the tools to find their God-given destiny, c) communicate a world impacting vision that people want to be a part of, d) pursue heart connections with the key people in our ministry, and e) increasingly empower people to be able to lead and train others.

2. **Help people become skilled in managing their time** – Train "specialists" who are in good relationship with you to equip your people to manage well their money, emotions, relationships, and time. All of these are important, but it could be argued that managing our time is the most important.

3. **Focus more on increasing people's ability to influence than on having specific ministries in your church** – Pastors are to primarily equip people, not create programs. We will have great ministries if we raise up leaders and influencers. When we combine equipping people with the following points of wisdom, we will increase the likelihood of people prioritizing the emphasis of the church: a) Ask for shorter commitments – like six to eight weeks for a small group or training emphasis. b) Group people according to their passions. c) Have meetings at more convenient times for people (lunch, right before other meetings, etc.). d) Empower people to minister in creative ways.

DECLARATIONS

- The people of our ministry have great priorities.
- People cannot wait to be involved in our efforts for kingdom advancement.
- We have many capable leaders and influencers that people gather to.

SCENARIO

Frank and Fran Faithful have been a great strength to Go Church through ministry and finances, but they have been having trouble with the new direction Pastor Sinclair Sincere is leading the church. Frank and Fran tell Pastor Sincere they believe God is telling them to go to On Fire Church across town. They say they just cannot buy in to everything that is happening, and they feel more comfortable at On Fire. The Faithfuls are the third family from the church to leave for On Fire Church in the last six months. If you were Pastor Sincere, how would you respond to the Faithfuls?

LIES ASSOCIATED WITH THIS SCENARIO

- My life and ministry are being ruined by people like the Faithfuls.
- No great pastor has ever have had anyone leave his or her church.
- I should speak negatively about this couple and shun them, and I also should call the new church they are attending a sheep-stealing church.
- God would never ask someone to leave the church I pastor.

LIFE AND LEADERSHIP CORE VALUES TO CONSIDER

55 I have an abundance mentality instead of a lack mentality.
48 My response to something is almost always more important than the something.
17 I thrive in uncertainty, difficulty, and unresolved situations because I have a "word" from the Lord.
33 I measure success by how many of our people are advancing the kingdom outside of the church walls.
52 I am a God-pleaser, not a people-pleaser.

DISCERNING WHAT GOD IS DEVELOPING IN ME

- I am learning to put my trust in the Lord and not in people.
- I have the opportunity to allow God to reaffirm the direction I am leading the church.
- I get to bless and maintain healthy relationships with people who leave the ministry I am leading.

HELP! I'M A PASTOR

QUESTIONS TO ASK BEFORE TAKING ACTION

1. What is my pattern of behavior and emotions when someone leaves my church?
2. What can I learn from this situation that may help prevent others from leaving?
3. Is there a concern about how this couple is leaving that I should address?
4. What is the Holy Spirit saying to me about my relationship with the church they are leaving for?
5. What is the word from the Lord to encourage and sustain me during this time?

PRACTICAL STEPS TO CONSIDER

1. **Take a long range view and strengthen your hope and love** – When people leave our churches, we are often challenged with lies that create feelings of failure, rejection, anger, fear, double-mindedness, and discouragement. Even so, this happening presents a great opportunity to grow in the abundance-mindsets that will ultimately attract people to us. "Poverty thinking" is behind many of the fears and doubts we face, but "prosperous soul thinking" produces genuine love and a heart to bless people who leave (because we are more concerned for their well-being than for the success of our church). This may be challenging in the moment, but as we grow in this mindset, it will reflect a health in our leadership that is rare and draws quality people to us.

2. **Realize sometimes it is good for people to leave** – Pastors at times hold on to people to the detriment of the church. We might be afraid of losing influencers or big givers, but often those people are actually holding back the greater increase of the ministry. When certain people leave, it can increase unity, freedom, and opportunities for others to minister and lessen emotional challenges for you and the leadership team.

3. **Keep growing** – There are two extreme reactions we can have when people leave – attack the one leaving or overly blame ourselves. Usually there is some truth on both sides, and therefore it is wisdom for us to find ways to improve what we are doing in our ministry at these times. We refuse to become people-pleasers, but we also refuse to stop growing and bettering what we do. When you are ready, get with your leadership team or other trusted people, and ask the Holy Spirit what He is saying to you through this.

DECLARATIONS

- My prosperous soul increasingly attracts quality people to our ministry.
- I have unusually healthy relationships with those who have left our church.
- God is our provider, not people.

SCENARIO

Rich N. Mercy is the senior leader at Getting Out of Crisis Fellowship. He has always had a great influence on "down and outers." He and his wife, Sharin, are incredible hope-bringers who are responsible for many homeless and addicted people getting free and becoming strong in life and ministry. Recently, Rich and Sharin have sensed God's leading to expand their ministry to the "up and uppers." He sees them as an unreached people group in his area. If you were Pastor Mercy, how would you move forward?

LIES ASSOCIATED WITH THIS SCENARIO

- Jesus loves the poor but dislikes those who have become rich.
- It is impossible for me to be influential with wealthy people.
- The same mindsets to reach the poor will also reach the rich.
- No ministry should make their main focus to reach the wealthy and influential.

LIFE AND LEADERSHIP CORE VALUES TO CONSIDER

18   In any people group my ministry wants to influence, I look for the "son of peace" (or "daughter of peace") to work through.

42   I am primarily a developer of leaders.

28   I regularly educate our people about our ministry's philosophy and process of decision making.

52   I am a God-pleaser, not a people-pleaser.

16   I embrace seasons of building trust in the eyes of those I lead.

DISCERNING WHAT GOD IS DEVELOPING IN ME

- I am learning to refrain from stereotyping any group of people.
- I have the opportunity to believe I can influence people in high places.
- I get to have compassion on a group of people who need Jesus.

QUESTIONS TO ASK BEFORE TAKING ACTION

1. What poverty beliefs influence me?
2. Do I believe God wants to radically bless my people financially? Why or why not?
3. What do I need to do differently to reach wealthy and influential people?
4. Do I believe it is possible to reach both poor and rich?

PRACTICAL STEPS TO CONSIDER

1. **Develop the belief that it would be ridiculous to not be connected with what you are doing** – There is a difference between pride and believing who God says we are. Abraham not only was blessed, but he was a blessing to whoever partnered with him. He was confident God's supernatural force of blessing would positively impact everything he did, everywhere he went, and everyone in his life (consider his attitude in Genesis 13 when he and Lot were deciding where to settle). Most Christians seem to have more faith we are cursed than blessed. Here is the good news to give us confidence we can think like Abraham: "Christ has redeemed us from the curse of the law, having become a curse for us… that the blessing of Abraham might come upon the Gentiles in Christ Jesus" (Galatians 3:13-14).

2. **Eliminate some of the reasons why people are not drawn to your ministry** – Some of these could be: a) chronic dysfunction in leadership team, b) "spirits" of poverty manifesting in church appearance and overall disorganization, c) church leaders primarily focusing on what the wealthy can do for the church instead of what the church can do for the wealthy, d) thinking all leaders/influencers in the church must have the same time commitments to church activities, and e) not having a plan to protect the privacy of the rich and famous.

3. **Believe and strategize for greater increase in your life and ministry** – The Parable of the Talents in Matthew 25 makes it clear we are designed for increase. Also, our Great Commission in Matthew 28 requires abundance because it is impossible to fulfill this assignment if we live in lack in resources and beliefs. As we become fully convinced of God's plan for us through these passages and others, our expectations of what we will experience in life and who will connect to us will go to higher levels. This faith will be a magnet for ideas and strategies which will bless ourselves and others.

DECLARATIONS

- I powerfully influence the rich and famous.
- Abundance mindsets are replacing poverty mindsets in our lives and ministry.
- God has made me a blessing to all who connect with me.

SCENARIO

Pastor Anita Dollar has a big vision for what her church will do in their city, but they are regularly lacking resources. She sees church members buying new cars, going on vacations, and wearing the latest styles, but she does not feel that people are giving their fair share in the offering. She set a budget this year with her elders, and the giving is less than the projected amount. She is feeling the pressure to raise money and is frustrated with her church people that they are not giving more. If you were Pastor Dollar, what would you do?

LIES ASSOCIATED WITH THIS SCENARIO

- There is nothing I can do to lead these people into greater generosity.
- Our people are basically greedy, stingy, and hate to give.
- If people just loved God more, our church would have all the money we need.
- It would be selfish to call people to a stronger financial commitment to the church.

LIFE AND LEADERSHIP CORE VALUES TO CONSIDER

12 I go the extra mile in honesty and in establishing accountability concerning how ministry money is handled.
13 I refuse to blame those I lead for the quality of our ministry.
45 I give generously in the areas where I have need.
47 I equip those I lead to be financially successful so they can be trusted with true spiritual riches.
50 I believe people want to do the right thing; therefore, my default belief is to give the benefit of the doubt to others.

DISCERNING WHAT IS BEING DEVELOPED IN ME

- I am learning to steward what I have as the first step to discipling nations.
- I have the opportunity to grow the muscles of endurance and trust.
- I get to have my prayer life and faith increase like never before.

QUESTIONS TO ASK BEFORE TAKING ACTION

1. What example am I (and my team) setting in personal finances and giving?
2. Do I believe that people love to give, or that they must be coerced to give?
3. Have I asked God for a strategy, or mentors to learn from, in this situation?
4. Who in our ministry can I partner with in prayer, wisdom, and faith to see greater financial victory for the church and those who attend?

PRACTICAL STEPS TO CONSIDER

1. **Remember: God is your ultimate source, not people** – God's resources are unlimited. Leaders can fall into the trap that some person is their source. People are just a resource that God can flow through to supply need and fulfill vision. Bill Hybels reminds leaders that "God is not just able to help, He is actually eager to help. The church is His bride… No one wants to see a church appropriately resourced more than God does" (*Courageous Leadership*, 98). Any fruitful or growing ministry will require resources. Since God is not tied to earth's economy, He has wisdom for His bride for finances.

2. **Be vision-driven rather than needs-driven** – People do not get excited to give to just pay the bills. People give to a vision that is making a difference. Consider doing an annual message on vision where you take time to paint pictures of the kingdom difference your church is called to make in your city and in the nations. Regularly give testimonies about how lives are changing in the church. Challenge yourself and key leaders to set the level of sacrifice in giving. Keep your church informed if there are financial challenges. (Paul Manwaring offers a Strategic Planning Toolkit that helps pastors and leaders discover the unique vision God has for their church.)

3. **Teach on giving, stewardship, and finances** – Teachers and leaders need to educate people about managing money, stewardship, tithing, and giving. Do a two to three week series on finances every year. January can be a good time to do this because people are naturally rethinking their budget. Follow up the sermon series on money with a budget planning workshop or class. (Dave Ramsey and Stephen DeSilva have great resources for this.) Bring in anointed guest speakers and use offering declarations.

DECLARATIONS

- Every time I give money, it becomes a military weapon in my hand. I turn those dollars into soldiers to advance the kingdom of God on planet earth.
- Our church is on a generosity rampage, seeking whom we can bless next.
- Every person in our church is debt free (including his or her house) and is abundantly generous.

SCENARIO

Pastor Peter Passive has recently decided to preach on a topic that is new and potentially controversial to some of his people. As he does so, Ronny Rebuker stands up and rebukes Pastor Passive publicly, claiming that what he is saying is demonic. He tells Peter he should repent. Pastor Passive is faced with a decision, and everyone is looking to him. If you were Pastor Passive, what would you do?

LIES ASSOCIATED WITH THIS SCENARIO

*   I need to yell and scream at Ronny so he (and everyone else) will know who is in charge in this meeting.
*   I must be doing something wrong if someone ever rebukes me publicly.
*   This is the end of the world for me because I am sure this has never happened to any other pastor.
*   I should not have any compassion or love for Ronny because there is obviously no hope for him.

LIFE AND LEADERSHIP CORE VALUES TO CONSIDER

63 Freedom does not mean that anything can happen.
52 I am a God-pleaser, not a people-pleaser.
60 God works everything together for good in my ministry.
64 I am careful in the words I use regarding those I am having difficulty with.
78 I realize the same environment that exposed a Judas also created eleven world changers.

DISCERNING WHAT GOD IS DEVELOPING IN ME

*   I am learning how to deal with confrontation in a healthy manner.
*   I have the opportunity to love people in difficult situations.
*   I get to realize that not everyone will agree with me, and it's okay.

QUESTIONS TO ASK BEFORE TAKING ACTION

1. Am I willing to take criticism for what I believe is right?
2. Can I speak from a place of love when being challenged?
3. What is happening corporately that I may need to address to make people feel safe?
4. Am I placing the fear of man above the fear of God?

PRACTICAL STEPS TO CONSIDER

1. **Keep your peace and keep focusing on Jesus** – As we remain calm, it will help our people stay calm. When strange things happen, people naturally look to their leader to know how they should react. As we (and our team) respond wisely, firmly, and with as much respect as possible for the rebuker, it will build confidence toward the leadership. When an incident like this is over, it is often a good idea to pray with love and humility in our hearts before proceeding with the service.

2. **Learn how to be firm, but gentle in handling difficult situations** – Some leaders won't deal with situations unless they are angry. It is like a parent who will only enforce rules if they have had enough disobedience and finally get mad. If this is our tendency, then the chances of us confronting a situation in an honoring way is slim. If someone rebukes you publicly and is disrupting the meeting, it is best to say something like, "I am so sorry you feel that way. We share your heart for preaching truth. It is clear though on this matter we disagree on what the Bible says. We would certainly be willing to talk with you after the service about your concerns."

3. **Select and train a security team for your church** – It is wisdom to have a plan ready for unexpected things that might happen in a church. Whether it is a Ronny Rebuker who feels compelled to correct perceived doctrinal wrongs, or a disgruntled ex-spouse who feels your church has taken sides in a divorce, there are plenty of reasons why a strategy needs to be developed for how to handle combative people. Many churches have people with law enforcement experience who would love to be a part of a security team that honors your core values.

DECLARATIONS

- I always respond in love and honor when challenged.
- I carry complete peace and wisdom when difficult situations arise.
- God always gives me the right words to say in high-pressured situations.

SCENARIO

Suzie Shabba and Danny Dynamite from Fire Church have been going around town "bringing revival" to local businesses. Suzie and Danny recently went into a local restaurant and announced in the middle of the restaurant that at Fire Church, Pastor Benny Bold said the church needs to demonstrate the power of God. They then proceed to start shaking and shouting in tongues to show that God is real. The owner of the restaurant becomes extremely upset as he notices some of his customers leaving. He calls Pastor Bold demanding that he do something about what has just happened. If you were Pastor Bold, what would you do?

LIES ASSOCIATED WITH THIS SCENARIO

* Because a mess was made in the name of my church, we can never have favor in our city.
* I should not care what the heathen restaurant owner thinks.
* We must make it a priority that no one in our city thinks poorly of our church.
* I should be embarrassed of Suzie and Danny for being such poor Christians.

LIFE AND LEADERSHIP CORE VALUES TO CONSIDER

48 My response to something is almost always more important than the something.
63 Freedom does not mean that anything can happen.
38 I pastor a city and region, not just a local church.
28 I regularly educate our people about our ministry's philosophy and process of decision making.
53 I help people understand how their behavior impacts others.

DISCERNING WHAT IS BEING DEVELOPED IN ME

* I am learning to love people in difficult situations.
* I have the opportunity to grow in understanding the hearts of people.
* I get to build bridges of understanding from the church to the marketplace.

QUESTIONS TO ASK BEFORE TAKING ACTION

1. Am I willing to take criticism for the move of the Spirit?
2. How can I use this to build a stronger relationship with Suzie and Danny?
3. How can we improve our training and accountability in our outreach ministry?
4. How can our ministry genuinely help the businesses in our city to succeed?

PRACTICAL STEPS TO CONSIDER

1. **Know that your response to your people's mistakes will greatly affect the quality of your relationships in your ministry** – When people make mistakes, it is a crucial moment, pregnant with potential for your relationship with them. If you make it clear they are more important than your reputation, then you increase the likelihood of having a deep heart connection and dynamic relationship with them. However if you become angry and send "you are messing up my life" messages to them, then the chances for a strong relationship diminish.

2. **Train your people to minister out on the streets with power and love** – One of the greatest things we can do is to inspire and equip people to bring "God encounters" to people outside of the church walls. Many ministries have been inspired by Kevin Dedmon's book, *The Ultimate Treasure Hunt*, to empower people to bring salvation, healing, and breakthrough to men and women in parks, stores, schools, and other places. (It is one of the greatest "highs" a Christian can have when they realize they can release the supernatural to others outside of the church.) Part of this training should also include teaching proper protocols for ministry such as honoring business owners and having genuine love for people.

3. **Do not be afraid of messes, but purpose to clean up those that happen** – "Where no oxen are, the trough is clean; but much increase comes by the strength of an ox" (Proverbs 14:4). If our goal in ministry is to never have a mess or apparent failure, we probably will not accomplish much. Those who succeed most seem to fail most. Babies make messes, and those going to higher levels of Christian living will make messes too. With that being said, leaders can help their people grow by helping them to apologize and make restitution for wrongs done. In the scenario above, one "mess cleaning solution" would be to apologize to the business owner, and for the church to write a check to cover any lost business that day and/or to bless the business owner.

DECLARATIONS

- I carry complete peace and wisdom when difficult situations arise.
- My level of love and honor for others remains the same despite how they act.
- I build bridges within my city that allow everyone to feel safe, valued, and heard.

SCENARIO

Pastor Ingrid Integrous looks at the calendar and realizes it is the time of year she loves and somewhat dreads – summer. While she is happy the winter cold has passed, she feels anxiety about a particular problem that comes with warmer weather – skimpy clothes being worn in church. Not only has she noticed church members wearing inappropriately small amounts of clothes, but she also has observed her staff is taking liberties with their dress as well. She does not want to be legalistic in addressing the clothing issue, but it has caused complaints from some of her elders and other members of the church. What would you do if you were Pastor Integrous?

LIES ASSOCIATED WITH THIS SCENARIO

- People will say I have a Pharisee spirit if I talk to them about their dress.
- The only solution is to have people show no skin except for their face and hands.
- I could have a problem with lust if I am bothered by inappropriate dress.
- There are no solutions so I should just let people wear whatever they want.

LIFE AND LEADERSHIP CORE VALUES TO CONSIDER

8   I pursue "buy-in" from leaders and key people involved before making a big decision.

70   I am more for things than I am against things.

63   Freedom does not mean that anything can happen.

35   I adapt my leadership and relational emphasis according to the culture I am in.

18   In any people group we want to influence, we look for the "son of peace" (or "daughter of peace") to work through.

DISCERNING WHAT IS BEING DEVELOPED IN ME

- I am learning to discern between religious tradition and godly principles for life.
- I have the opportunity to discern what the deeper issues behind matters are.
- I get to grow in my ability to troubleshoot sensitive matters.

QUESTIONS TO ASK BEFORE TAKING ACTION

1. Do people I trust agree this is a problem?
2. How does our geographical location and ministry emphasis affect this?
3. What is the difference between legalism and healthy, godly standards?
4. How can we establish vision for people regarding purity and modesty?

PRACTICAL STEPS TO CONSIDER

1. **Develop a strong discipleship ministry for men and women** – Men and women have unique needs and roles in life; therefore, it is wise to regularly equip each gender to understand how to navigate through the particular challenges each will face. As this is proactively done, it will lessen the need to try to fix problems in areas such as clothing choices. Also, this distinct emphasis in men and women's issues will develop leaders who can help increase godly standards in the ministry. There are many wonderful teaching resources to help in this discipleship, and there are thriving ministries to men and women that can help as well.

2. **Address modesty issues in an overall strategy of moral purity for your congregation** – Because immodesty often starts as a heart issue or a lack of understanding, it is unwise to isolate immodest attire away from the bigger issue of moral health in sexual and purity issues. The greater the understanding that people have concerning purity in relationships, the greater the likelihood they will understand the wisdom in dressing modestly. Many churches have a moral purity emphasis which creates a culture of intentionality in different areas, including helping people make powerful choices in what to wear. Mothers of teenagers will be especially glad if you give support to them in this area. Note: We highly recommend the materials from Moral Revolution for this purpose (www.moralrevolution.com).

3. **Keep majoring in majors, not in minors** – It is vital to: a) be more for things than against things, b) to release the kingdom more than trying to stop the devil, c) to speak about our biblical identities more than talking about conduct (inspiring change through vision rather than "do this to be a good Christian"), and d) to use humor to open eyes to higher levels of living rather than guilt and condemnation. Also, consider cultural factors in developing your philosophy – a leader who has a ministry on a beach in Hawaii will have a different mindset than someone pastoring in Iceland.

DECLARATIONS

- I am a great communicator in difficult situations.
- I am a standard-bearer in every area of my ministry.
- I address sensitive subjects with grace, love, vision, and wisdom.

SCENARIO

Quantum Glory Church has been having great services. People are being overcome with God's presence during worship: they are weeping, confessing their sins, being healed, and having transformational encounters. The church has gone for weeks without a sermon because of these happenings. Pastor R. U. Fild loves what is happening, but wonders if it is a good idea to not have a sermon for that many Sundays. If you were Pastor Fild, what would you do?

LIES ASSOCIATED WITH THIS SCENARIO

*   The most important thing a pastor does in a service is preach the sermon.
*   If the sermon is not preached, it is an incomplete service.
*   Because the sermon is unimportant, it should only be preached if God is not moving in the service.
*   The anointing of God carries greater weight than the truth of God for setting people free.

LIFE AND LEADERSHIP CORE VALUES TO CONSIDER

26   I err on the side of allowing too much Holy Spirit activity, rather than too little.

28   I regularly educate our people about our ministry's philosophy and process of decision making.

29   I purposely do not overly plan meetings, so there will be an increased likelihood of a "suddenly" of God happening.

46   The anointing brings great breakthrough, but it is hearing and believing truth that makes us free.

62   I understand the "times and seasons" of my ministry and what I am supposed to emphasize.

DISCERNING WHAT GOD IS DEVELOPING IN ME

*   I am learning to let go of controlling meetings too much.
*   I have the opportunity to discern what season our church is in.
*   I get to grow in letting the Holy Spirit lead me in my decision making.

QUESTIONS TO ASK BEFORE TAKING ACTION

1. What other tools besides the sermon can help my people be anchored in Scripture?

2. What is the fruit of these powerful encounters people are having – is there increased hunger for discipleship and the Word?

3. Is there a mindset in my people that if the sermon is preached, the Holy Spirit is not moving powerfully?

4. Could I preach before worship or at another time?

5. Who do I trust who can help me know the times and seasons of our ministry?

PRACTICAL STEPS TO CONSIDER

1. **Seize your times of special visitation** – Jesus wept over Jerusalem and said, "If you had known, even you, especially in this your day, the things that make for your peace!" (Luke 19:42). He said they had a special time of opportunity that they did not recognize. We too will be presented with times of unique outpourings to be embraced and pursued. Ask God for a heart to see and seize these times.

2. **Follow the Acts 2 model of experiencing and then explaining** – The 120 had a "suddenly" experience in Acts 2. The Holy Spirit invaded their meeting. Things got out of control in a good way. The disciples did not stop what was going on but flowed with it (even though it was totally new). It was so powerful that it became known to outsiders. These manifestations were criticized by those outside the experience. Peter rose up and preached a great sermon, giving explanation to what was happening. This Acts 2 model is good to meditate on when we experience ongoing "suddenlies."

3. **Meet and pray regularly with a group of leaders who are diversely gifted, who can help you recognize and lead special seasons of visitation** – It is the wise leader who develops a team around him or her to help interpret what is happening in meetings and to help in determining future direction. This group should include people of different giftings, but all need to have a heart to see people encounter God powerfully, even if at times it looks messy.

DECLARATIONS

- I lead a church where people regularly have life-changing encounters with God.

- My preaching and teaching cause signs and wonders to occur.

- I have great wisdom in leading church meetings.

SCENARIO

Senior Leader Ben Blue of I AM Church loves to preach and has a real gift to teach and usher in the presence of God. Even though this is true, Pastor Blue's disorganization and lack of communication is creating frustration for Bobby Better, his associate pastor. Bobby is starting to believe Pastor Blue is lazy and thinks he can do a better job at leading the church than him. Some people in the church have come to Bobby and said they wish he was the senior pastor. If you were Bobby, what would you do?

LIES ASSOCIATED WITH THIS SCENARIO

- Speaking to my pastor about any concerns would be dishonoring.
- God refuses to use leaders who have any weaknesses.
- Because I can see that my pastor's faults are causing problems in the church, it is obvious I would be a better pastor than him.
- God has no other purpose in this situation except for getting Pastor Blue fixed.

LIFE AND LEADERSHIP VALUES TO CONSIDER

14 I am more concerned about building people than I am concerned about building a ministry.

37 My faithfulness in small things opens doors for bigger opportunities.

53 I help people understand how their behavior impacts others.

43 I am honoring in attitudes and words I have about those in authority over me (even when I disagree with them).

39 I am more focused on my personal growth than in bringing change to those I am called to influence.

DISCERNING WHAT IS BEING DEVELOPED IN ME

- I am learning how to support another leader while continuing to grow in my own life, ministry, and vision.
- I have the opportunity to understand God's timing and wisdom like never before.
- I get to grow in my relationship with the leader God has called me to support.

QUESTIONS TO ASK BEFORE TAKING ACTION

1. Is my heart right toward my pastor, or am I walking in pride and selfish ambition?
2. How much trust have I built in the eyes of Pastor Blue, and what can I do to help him trust my perspective more?
3. What are the most important things I can do to help Pastor Blue?
4. What are my trusted spiritual mentors saying to me about this?
5. How can I best bring increased health to our church?

PRACTICAL STEPS TO CONSIDER

1. **Reaffirm you are where God wants you to be** – We can put up with a lot of uncertainty and outward non-success if we have a confidence we are where God wants us to be. Nobody is in a perfect situation, so every Christian leader must base his decisions, emotions, and conclusions on what God has said, not on whether circumstances are good or not. Jesus said, "Man shall not live by bread alone but by every word that proceeds from the mouth of God" (Matthew 4:4). We truly live when we identify and stand on what God has spoken to us.

2. **Realize that how you behave and think under a leader now will sow seeds for how people will behave and think under your future leadership** – "Give, and it will be given to you... for with the same measure that you use, it will be measured back to you" (Luke 6:38). The context of this verse is not about finances but about attitudes (forgiving, condemning, and judging). This is sobering and inspiring for our relationships. Especially as leaders, we are called to serve. Another verse to help guide our attitudes and actions in this situation is, "Whatever you want men to do to you, do also to them" (Matthew 7:7).

3. **Become a problem solver, not a self-promoter or a complainer** – Wherever God calls us, we are to become part of the solution, not part of the problem – even if it involves the senior pastor. Again, every environment we find ourselves in will have some disappointments and frustrations. These challenges are our opportunity to pull on the Holy Spirit within us to bring solutions and to demolish any strongholds we might have of self-promotion and complaining. As we do, it will be impossible for good doors not to open for us in the future.

DECLARATIONS

·   My presence in a ministry creates positive change for every life and situation.
·   Because of my attitude, love for Jesus, and work ethic, my pastor wishes he or she had fifty people like me on the leadership team.
·   I am full of courage, love, and wisdom in dealing with church problems.

SCENARIO

It has been months since Pastor Itta Hasta Happennow came back from the conference where he received a dozen prophetic words about the "more of God" invading his congregation. Included in these words were promises of signs and wonders, healings, and manifestations of the glory of God, so powerful that people would come from many places to encounter it. Despite pressing in for months, nothing is outwardly happening. In fact, people are beginning to leave the church because things are not happening in the manner Pastor Happennow said it would. Itta is doing everything he knows to do, but nothing seems to be changing. How would you handle this situation?

LIES ASSOCIATED WITH THIS SCENARIO

• Breakthrough cannot happen because of the poor quality of people in the church.

• The prophetic words were probably an exaggeration of what God really wanted to do.

• Revival only happens where I am not present.

• If it seems like nothing is happening, then nothing is happening.

LIFE AND LEADERSHIP CORE VALUES TO CONSIDER

33 I measure success by how many of our people are advancing the kingdom outside of the church walls.

80 I regularly share testimonies of God's goodness and power as a strategy to bring our ministry into its fullness.

13 I refuse to blame those I lead for the quality of our ministry.

49 I am "sent" by trustworthy people into the ministry I have, and I continue to pursue accountability with them.

23 I live and demonstrate the gospel supernaturally as a model for others.

DISCERNING WHAT IS BEING DEVELOPED IN ME

• I am learning to pastor my church through disappointments.

• I have the opportunity to understand that personal frustration is one of the biggest enemies of revival.

• I get to celebrate progress and not just perfection.

QUESTIONS TO ASK BEFORE TAKING ACTION

• What is God doing that we can celebrate?

• Who can help me know what to do?

• Do I have wrong beliefs that could be hindering spiritual breakthrough?

• Is there something God is telling us to do or repent of?

• How long am I willing to press in for God's glory to manifest in our midst?

PRACTICAL STEPS TO CONSIDER

1. **Create opportunities for your leaders and your people to encounter God** – a) Find a group of people who are spiritually hungry and seek God together. Wait in His presence, worship, prophesy, review past prophecies, pray for each other, respond to Holy Spirit impulses, and hear the "now word" for lives and the ministry. b) Take your leadership team to places where what you desire is happening. c) Bring in guest speakers to spark spiritual awakening. d) Build a culture where people take kingdom power and love outside of the church walls to heal, prophesy, evangelize, love, etc. Don't wait for it to happen in the church sanctuary.

2. **Be thankful and do not despise the day of small beginnings** – Focusing on what God is doing rather than what does not seem to be happening is a crucial mindset if we are going to lead in a healthy way. Regularly sharing testimonies from the lives of your people and from people you know will put more "wood" on the fire of revival. Also, as we avoid frustration and remain radically thankful, we will model a balance of pursuing Him and resting in His promises.

3. **Encounter God powerfully yourself** – One person touched by the power of God can change a nation, a city, and most definitely a church. The Bible is full of ordinary people who did extraordinary things because they had a supernatural encounter with God. As we prioritize our own transformation through desire, faith, impartation from others, risk taking, and receiving His love, we will have a breakthrough that creates a breakthrough for those we lead.

DECLARATIONS

• God is radically moving in our church and ministry, and He is doing more than I can see right now.

• The prophetic words over our church will come to pass.

• My spiritual hunger and personal revival bring breakthrough to everyone around me.

SCENARIO

Mr. and Mrs. Hypersons have four sons and two daughters. They attend Smile for Jesus Church. The Hypersons' children are known for being loud, extremely energetic, and often disruptive. It is not infrequent for the younger Hypersons son, Expresso, to wander around church during the sermon – sometimes walking up on the platform while Pastor Keepa De Peace is preaching. Mr. and Mrs. Hyperson seem to think it is cute when Expresso gets on the stage. Pastor De Peace feels frustrated about what is going on, but does not want to upset this family. If you were Pastor De Peace, what would you do?

LIES ASSOCIATED WITH THIS SCENARIO

*   Children should not be seen or heard at church.
*   It would be dishonoring and unloving to mention any concerns I have to these parents.
*   Children who misbehave in church have no future as a Christian.
*   We should ignore the children's misbehavior and hope it stops.

LIFE AND LEADERSHIP CORE VALUES TO CONSIDER

77 We provide regular training and education on key life skills.
63 Freedom does not mean that anything can happen.
64 I am careful in the words I use regarding those I am having a difficulty with.
58 I confront people with love and inspire them to grow by reminding them of their destiny.
14 I am more concerned about building people than I am concerned about building a ministry.

DISCERNING WHAT GOD IS DEVELOPING IN ME

*   I am learning how to have patience for those around me.
*   I have the opportunity to create life-giving standards, not just rules.
*   I get to grow in my ability to confront with love and honor.

QUESTIONS TO ASK BEFORE TAKING ACTION

1.   Do I have a fear of making people angry if I share concerns with them?
2.   How can we train our church family to respond well to such situations?
3.   What steps can we take to improve our ministry to children during the services?
4.   How can we be a special blessing to the Hypersons?

PRACTICAL STEPS TO CONSIDER

1. **Constantly improve your children's ministry** – A church that wants to increase its impact cannot ignore its ministry to children. For some ministries it may seem impossible to take forward steps, but there is always something that can be done. One suggestion is to meet with key people in your ministry and ask, "What are five things our ministry can do right now to be more child-friendly? How can we more effectively influence children?" The Holy Spirit is faithful to speak. As we move forward with what we can do, it will create a momentum for greater things to be done. (We share in another part of this book ideas of how to see your children's ministry grow.)

2. **Proactively help parents who are new to your ministry understand your children's ministry and your church protocols** – A well-trained greeter can spot new families with children easily. It is best to be intentional about letting them know about the nursery and children's ministry. Also, the greeter can say something like, "If you choose to have your younger children with you in the service, there is a special cry room in the back if you find you need it in the middle of service." If you are proactive in this, it will lessen the amount of uncomfortable reactive decisions and conversations you will need to have.

3. **Err on the side of letting too much happen in your church, but do not let it turn into a dysfunction** – Having a concern about the quality of your relationship with the parents will inspire grace and patience with such things as children wandering around church during the service. (Hopefully the people in your ministry also carry a healthy concern for relationship). However, it is one thing to have it happen a week or two, but in most situations it is a dysfunction to have it happen regularly. You not only want to love the parents, but you also want to love your congregation by creating an environment in which they can grow.

DECLARATIONS

- I get a greater revelation and impartation of my identity as a son or daughter of God through interacting with the children of my church.
- I am a gracious loving leader who makes excellent decisions.
- We have a flourishing children's ministry.

SCENARIO

Pastor Phileo Agape leads Grace Church. Pastor Agape's ministry on the love of God has changed many lives, but some in the church believe Phileo does not confront wrong behaviors in the congregation strongly enough. One man, Stan Dard Bearer, became very adamant about this when a teenage girl in the youth group became pregnant. "Pastor, unless you become firmer in dealing with sin in this church, we are going to have more problems like this. There is so much emphasis on God's unconditional love that no one takes responsibility for their actions! We should discuss holiness!" If you were Pastor Agape, how would you respond?

LIES ASSOCIATED WITH THIS SCENARIO

- My main job as a pastor is to make everyone feel good about themselves no matter what they are doing.
- Great church leaders should use the fear of punishment as the primary motivator to stop sin.
- If I confront a behavior and label it as wrong, people will think I am legalistic or hateful.
- The only way to show I am not soft on sin is to become expressively angry.

LIFE AND LEADERSHIP CORE VALUES TO CONSIDER

63 Freedom does not mean that anything can happen.
66 I motivate people through vision instead of guilt and manipulation.
67 The people of our ministry have clear, healthy avenues to share concerns they have about the church or me.
58 I confront people with love and inspire them to grow by reminding them of their destiny.
77 We provide regular training and education on key life skills.

DISCERNING WHAT GOD IS DEVELOPING IN ME

- I am learning how to increase people's confidence in my leadership.
- I have the opportunity to strengthen my convictions about how people really change.
- I get to develop deeper connections with spiritual mothers and fathers.

QUESTIONS TO ASK BEFORE TAKING ACTION

1. Is there an emphasis on law that is actually causing sin to manifest?
2. What can I learn from other leaders on balancing the "grace message" with a culture that confronts people who persist in wrong choices or lifestyles?
3. How much does the fear of man affect how I approach situations like this?
4. How can I preach God's love and still emphasize a healthy fear of God?
5. How can I grow in leading people into godly repentance?

PRACTICAL STEPS TO CONSIDER

1. **Continually proclaim the finished work of the cross and the true identity of the believer** – It is impossible to consistently do what we do not believe we are. If we try to act righteous, but believe we are a sinner, then that belief becomes our biggest problem – and we will actually sin by faith. Because "faith comes by hearing" (Romans 10:17, Galatians 3:5), our main role in preaching and teaching is to share the good news of the gospel about what Jesus has done and who we are in Him. Just like the Apostle Paul, if we are really preaching grace, we will probably be accused of giving permission for people to sin.

2. **Assess how people live out what you preach** – It is enlightening to see how people interpret our message. I (Steve) share often on not speaking death with our words. I noticed a number of people under my ministry interpreted this truth in a way that caused them to live in denial and be unauthentic in relationships. This feedback caused me to adjust how I presented this revelation about words.

3. **Restore people, but also confront any tendency toward covering up or excusing blatant sin** – Galatians 6:1 reveals "spiritual people" will restore those "overtaken in any trespass." This verse and Matthew 18:15-17 imply that leaders will not ignore but address those in the church family who are compromising clear biblical standards. These conversations are to be done with love and humility for the individual, but it also will send the message that the influencers in the church must live a life of integrity, purity, and love. Note: We certainly are not going to confront every poor choice people make, but as the discipleship process advances with individuals, we will realize we cannot ignore blatant sin or doctrines that give license to unbiblical lifestyles or choices.

DECLARATIONS

*   I lead a ministry where people are set free from sinful habits.
*   The leaders in our church walk in integrity, love, and purity.
*   I am not afraid to confront people who need to be confronted.

SCENARIO

Senior Pastor Keep N. Peoples leads We Are Family Ministries. They are a church of about 100 people, and they frequently have visitors who visit their services and special meetings. A common comment from someone visiting is, "Wow, God is really here. We were so blessed to be here." Unfortunately, the vast majority of these excited people never return. Recently Cap A. Chino came to a meeting for the first time and said, "I have found my church family! I want to be a member." Cap never returned. Pastor Peoples wonders what the problem is. If you were Pastor Peoples, what would you do?

LIES ASSOCIATED WITH THIS SCENARIO

- There is nothing we can do to increase the likelihood visitors will become part of our church family.
- It is all up to me as the pastor to help people want to be a part of our church.
- People who pastor and disciple are not as important as people who are speakers and worship leaders.
- Everyone who visits our church is supposed to be a part of our church.

LIFE AND LEADERSHIP CORE VALUES TO CONSIDER

14 I am more concerned about building people than I am concerned about building a ministry.
18 In any people group our ministry wants to influence, I look for the "son of peace" (or "daughter of peace") to work through.
33 I measure success by how many of our people are advancing the kingdom outside of the church walls.
38 I pastor a city and region, not just a local church.
68 I have a strong ability to make people feel needed, valued, and loved in our ministry as opposed to them feeling used.

DISCERNING WHAT IS GOD IS DEVELOPING IN ME

- I am learning how to meet the needs of people without compromising our core values.
- I have the opportunity to see our church from a visitor's perspective.
- I get to find higher ways to connect with and bless people who have visited our ministry.

HELP! I'M A PASTOR

QUESTIONS TO ASK BEFORE TAKING ACTION

- Is there a pattern for why people are not returning?
- How can we improve our visitor retention without becoming people-pleasers?
- Who in our ministry is uniquely gifted to help in this matter?
- Do I have an unhealthy need to pastor a large church so I will feel successful?

PRACTICAL STEPS TO CONSIDER

1. **Clarify your purpose as a church** – We are to be purpose-driven, not attendance-driven. Our main goal is not increased numbers, but increased impact in lives and increased impact in every sphere of society. It is important to reaffirm the vision of the ministry before putting a strong emphasis on keeping visitors. It is also wise to remember not every visitor will be called to be part of your ministry.

2. **Address obvious reasons people do not stay** – Focusing on keeping visitors creates good pressure to move into greater excellence in how things are done and how people are cared for. Consider correcting reasons why people may not stay. These include: a) not having a good system for collecting contact information from visitors, b) unfriendly people who project "We are a members-only church," c) not having a trained and welcoming team of greeters, d) little or no follow-up of those who visit, and e) a lack of excellence in practical things including bathrooms, parking lots, and punctuality. Here is a tip for smaller to mid-size churches: Designate a person to work with one of your key leaders to note who is in church and who is not. Have them find life-giving, non-guilt causing ways to send "You were missed, and you are important to us" messages.

3. **Find ways to serve every visitor whether they ever return or not** – When someone visits our ministry, our goal is to become a strength in their life, not to get them to come to our church. This mindset brings freedom in our relationship with them, and actually increases the likelihood they will stay. Enhance connection with them by letting them know periodically you are praying for them, by having a good social media ministry and web presence that allows them to feel informed and connected, and by finding practical ways to help their family life, finances, careers, and emotional well-being.

DECLARATIONS

- People radically encounter God in our services.
- Everyone who comes into contact with our ministry is loved and equipped.
- Our ministry is becoming healthier and healthier.

SCENARIO

Ken De Keen was an enthusiastic member of Hope Church. The leadership of the church was at first impressed with his drive and passion. As time went on, Ken became disappointed in the church. He voiced his disagreement with the leadership and started sharing his frustrations with others. He eventually organized a meeting about the problems in the church. The meeting did not go well because most sided with leadership, and some even rebuked Ken. Feeling humiliated and shamed, he decided it was time to leave the church. When he left, he sent an email to everyone in the church saying negative things about the leadership. Pastor Lettuce Gettalong was confused about this. What would you do?

LIES ASSOCIATED WITH THIS SCENARIO

- Nothing like this has ever happened in any impactful church.
- The most important goal of a church is to make sure everyone is happy.
- There is no hope for Ken.
- If someone becomes angry, I should immediately let him have his way.

LIFE AND LEADERSHIP CORE VALUES TO CONSIDER

20 I proactively anticipate challenges that could occur in the future.

41 I decrease gossip in our ministry by setting the example of speaking directly with the people that I have a problem with and inviting them to speak directly with me.

50 I believe people want to do the right thing; therefore, my default belief is to give the benefit of the doubt to others.

58 I confront people with love and inspire them to grow by reminding them of their destiny.

76 I purpose to communicate sensitive matters with people face to face and not through text or e-mail.

DISCERNING WHAT GOD IS DEVELOPING IN ME

- I am learning to lead when someone is vocal in their displeasure of me.
- I have the opportunity to decrease relationship breakdowns in the church.
- I get to keep my peace and love when someone angrily leaves the church.

QUESTIONS TO ASK BEFORE TAKING ACTION

1. What could I have done to avoid this happening?
2. What is causing Ken to be disgruntled? Does Ken have a valid point?
3. How can we help the congregation know the truth in the situation without bashing Ken?
4. Who does Ken respect in the church who could help him?
5. How can we keep Ken in the church family while keeping the family safe?

PRACTICAL STEPS TO CONSIDER

1. **Train your people how to handle conflict and disagreement** – Many of our people simply do not know how to process hurt and disagreement in a healthy way or how to handle someone who is angry and accusatory. The wise pastor's teaching is very practical in answering questions such as, "What should I do if I get an email slandering leaders or others?" and "What should I do if I strongly feel leadership is leading the church in the wrong direction?" These topics can be addressed in special emphasis teachings and in sprinkled in messages throughout the year.

2. **Recommit to restoring those who have fallen** – "Brethren, if a man is overtaken in any trespass, you who are spiritual restore such a one in a spirit of gentleness, considering yourself lest you also be tempted" (Galatians 6:1). One of the signs of being spiritual is the ability to restore people. We start the restoration process by admitting any wrongs we have done in the relationship. Then we exercise loving firmness to help the person clean up their mess through repentance and seeking forgiveness.

3. **Address backbiting and negative emails** – If an individual refuses to correct his or her wrongs, then the church leadership needs to consider how to respond. The action taken will be determined by: a) how much unity and trust for leadership is in the church, b) Is the leadership team strong enough to handle this themselves? c) How influential is the individual? If an official action needs to be taken, consider having a church family meeting or sending an email acknowledging the situation and inviting people with questions to meet with you. Whatever you do, be very careful what you say publicly or write in emails.

DECLARATIONS

- My first response is love, restoration, and reconciliation.
- I do not need people to think like me for me to love them.
- I am a great leader and make great decisions.

SCENARIO

New Wine Church has a once a month Sunday evening Fire Meeting. These are services of extended worship, ministry to the sick, and powerful personal prayer. The Fire Meetings have been very impactful with miracles and breakthroughs, especially through the prayers of Val Cano and Tim Pestuous. These two have great faith and boldness to see the supernatural released, and they are eager to play a more important role for the Fire Meetings and in New Wine Church. Pastor Phil U. Moore loves what is happening through Val and Tim, but he is concerned because they both battle addictive behaviors and other lifestyle issues. If you were Phil, what would you do?

LIES ASSOCIATED WITH THIS SCENARIO

- The most outwardly anointed people should always be the leaders in church.
- Someone with obvious lifestyle problems should never be allowed to pray for others.
- People's behaviors do not matter as long as miracles happen through them.
- If Jesus had real discernment, He would never have had Peter on his leadership team.

LIFE AND LEADERSHIP CORE VALUES TO CONSIDER

22 I pursue relationships with the strong influencers in places I am called to lead.
26 I err on the side of allowing too much Holy Spirit activity, rather than too little.
14 I am more concerned about building people than I am concerned about building a ministry.
32 I "date" people in key ministry relationships before "marrying" them with a title.
66 I motivate people through vision instead of guilt and manipulation.

DISCERNING WHAT GOD IS DEVELOPING IN ME

- I am learning how to balance the need for people to feel safe with the need to have powerful, unpredictable moves of the Holy Spirit.
- I have the opportunity to grow in my leading revival type meetings.
- I get to increase my ability to communicate at a high level with anointed people who are struggling.

QUESTIONS TO ASK BEFORE TAKING ACTION

1. How can I deepen my relationship with these catalytic people?
2. How teachable are they? How much do they trust me?
3. What does my leadership team say about what is happening?
4. What do they need to do so I can have greater confidence in them?
5. How can I help people in our congregation embrace people who are at times "loose cannons?"

PRACTICAL STEPS TO CONSIDER

1. **Clearly communicate the difference between being an anointed person and being a leader** – Those with a special ability to release the supernatural can create a great meeting, but those walking in anointed leadership can create a movement. We certainly celebrate those who perform miracles, but it is wise to not give the impression that they are automatically leaders in your ministry because they do so. The anointed influencers of the ministry need to be directed to participate in the church's leadership development program so they can go to the next level of their influence.

2. **Value healthy, proactive communication** – Pursue relationship with these key influencers. Be excited about their heart to bring freedom to others. Build vision in them for where God is taking them. Help them understand how their current season fits into their prophetic destiny of leading others in a significant way. Tell them – "Where you are going, you cannot take this tendency with you." Work with them to develop a plan to deal with lifestyle issues. Some may not respond well to this process, but it is better to know that early on in the relationship to avoid future complications.

3. **Develop a strong ministry training program** – Many churches have ministry teams who are trained in the prophetic, leading people to Christ, physical healing, and in basic protocols of personal ministry to others. This training helps establish consistent doctrinal views and accountability for those used regularly in healing, miracles, and in releasing gifts of the Holy Spirit. Asking anointed influencers to participate in this structure is a good opportunity to help them be part of the overall team and not just be a "lone ranger."

DECLARATIONS

- People radically encounter God in our services.
- I am able to lead all kinds of people who flow in the anointing.
- Our ministry has well trained and effective ministry teams.

SCENARIO

Pastor Ree Leaser of Faith Church was thrilled to send Pash Ion across the country to Releasing the Spirit Ministry School (RSMS), a school that is impacting the world. RSMS is part of Risen Temple, and their senior pastor, Dino Mite, is a strong apostolic leader with international influence whom Pash respects much. When Pash returned home, he quickly became frustrated with Pastor Leaser and what he perceived to be a low level of spiritual life at Faith Church. Pash has been known to compare Faith Church with Risen Temple. He recently told Pastor Leaser, "The people here need more spiritual fire. Dino says you must pray until the glory falls. Pastor, I think you should read this book by Apostle Mite." If you were Ree, how would you handle this?

LIES ASSOCIATED WITH THIS SCENARIO

- Dissatisfied people in a congregation are always sent by the devil to torment pastors.
- If we do not do everything like a mega, revival church, then we have a bad church.
- I am obviously petty and insecure to let this bother me.
- There is nothing positive that can come out of this.

LIFE AND LEADERSHIP CORE VALUES TO CONSIDER

11   I recognize the tendency that current moves of God are often persecuted by those impacted by a previous move of God.

25   I believe people's negative qualities are usually immature characteristics of positive qualities in their life.

28   I regularly educate our people about our ministry's philosophy and process of decision making.

44   I seek to listen and understand before I seek to be heard and understood.

53   I help people understand how their behavior impacts others.

DISCERNING WHAT GOD IS DEVELOPING IN ME

- I am learning how to listen to and guide our people who are frustrated with my leadership.
- I have the opportunity to grow in confidence and the ability to communicate what God has told me.
- I get to help our church love and relate to a zealot who sometimes does not use wisdom.

QUESTIONS TO ASK BEFORE TAKING ACTION

1. How deep is my relationship with this person?
2. What things is he saying that seem to be the Lord speaking to us?
3. How much is he negatively impacting the church?
4. Who at the ministry school might be able to help with this?
5. How can I father this person through this season of his life?

PRACTICAL STEPS TO CONSIDER

1. **Approach this with love, wisdom, and a "word" from the Lord** – There are two extremes in approaching this situation. You could resist new things God wants to do in your midst, or you could become insecure and forget what God has already told you. In this situation, it would be best to strengthen your relationship with this person, listen to his heart, give him insight into your vision, invite him (if appropriate) to work with you in taking steps toward the legitimate things he is mentioning, and redirect him as necessary.

2. **Learn to hear truth through unlikely, and at times prickly, sources** – God has been known to use unusual vessels to speak into our lives (like donkeys!). Not everyone who brings truth and correction to us will be a nicely polished, compassionate and clear communicator. Some may be battling bitterness, others may be immature, and a few might have obvious faults. Clearly, we are not to allow ourselves to regularly be a dumping ground for someone's constant negativity or criticism – nor are we to become people-pleasers. It is a good idea to ask God what truth might be present in the criticism others have of you.

3. **Develop healthy relationships with apostolic ministries** – Every church and every pastor need relationships with influential or apostolic ministries. If you are going to fly like an eagle, you need to "hang out" with eagles. As God shows you what these connections are to be, take steps to allow their breakthrough to become yours: a) Celebrate the good things God is doing there. b) Prioritize your relationship with them in your calendar commitments (conferences you attend, guest speakers you have, etc.). c) Build relationship with someone there. d) Encourage them and help them fulfill their vision. e) Give feedback on how their ministry can improve in its connection to ministries like yours.

DECLARATIONS

- I minister successfully to those who are frustrated.
- I have great relationships with influential and apostolic leaders and ministries.
- I am a confident leader who can hear the word of the Lord through unlikely sources.

SCENARIO

"Oh, Pastor Superior, we are elated to be here. It is so much better than Faithful Church, where we just left. In just two weeks of attending, we know we want to become members here. Your people are so friendly, and your ministry is like nothing we have ever experienced. This is a great church! I cannot wait to tell the other unhappy ones at Faithful Church about this place. Pastor T. Edious isn't as anointed as you, and I can tell you are a lover of people, not controlling like him." If you were Pastor Superior, what should you do?

LIES ASSOCIATED WITH THIS SCENARIO

- This is obviously the best thing that has ever happened in my ministry.
- I should label this person as a church hopper and flee from him.
- I should rejoice when I hear other churches are struggling.
- God would never have a person leave one church to attend another.

LIFE AND LEADERSHIP CORE VALUES TO CONSIDER

9   I build a culture of feedback in my ministry that I lead by example.
14   I am more concerned about building people than I am concerned about building a ministry.
53   I help people understand how their behavior impacts others.
27   I process unverified information about others in a healthy way.
21   When people are struggling in life, I first seek to increase their connection to the Lord.

DISCERNING WHAT GOD IS DEVELOPING IN ME

- I am learning how to build the kingdom rather than just my local church.
- I have the opportunity to grow in love, humility, and wisdom as I relate to this person.
- I get to strengthen my attitudes and relationships with other churches and leaders.

QUESTIONS TO ASK BEFORE TAKING ACTION

1. How healthily do I process praise or criticism toward me?
2. What would cause me to ask someone to reconcile with their former church?
3. What would cause me to speak to the former pastor of a new person in my ministry?
4. How can we help new people who have been legitimately wounded by a church?

PRACTICAL STEPS TO CONSIDER

1. **Don't ignore your people's previous church relationships** – Just as someone considering a romantic relationship would be foolish to not know the person's history in relationships, a leader would also be unwise to be unfamiliar with how a potentially key person has related with former pastors and church leaders. Certainly you don't want to hold someone to their past, but understanding their tendencies and history will most likely be beneficial in your relationship with them. As you become aware of this, you will at times help new attendees clean up messes they made when they left past churches.

2. **Treat other churches and other pastors as you would want to be treated** – A pastor once said to another pastor, "I won't believe everything I hear about you, so please don't believe everything you hear about me." This illustrates the Golden Rule, which is a good guide for your relationships with other ministries. Some ways to do this are: a) Give the benefit of the doubt. b) Pursue relationships. c) Establish a reputation that you are a genuine kingdom-minded pastor who sincerely wants other ministries to succeed. These steps may be more challenging in urban areas, but you can still find ways to become for others what you need yourself.

3. **Be diligent to train your people in decision making and having healthy relationships with their church** – There are few greater skills you can equip your people with than how to make good decisions. It is also important to help your people understand that being a consistent part of a ministry fellowship is part of God's plan for them to grow personally and corporately. In your teachings, include wisdom about how to leave a church in a healthy way. These truths will help set a culture in your ministry, which will positively impact new people who come.

DECLARATIONS

- I have great love and wisdom for new people who come to our church.
- I am a catalyst for good relationships between churches in my area.
- I equip my people to become great decision makers and to do relationships well.

SCENARIO

Pastor M.T. Vessel pastors True Blue Ministries. He has been in this position for 25 years in their church of 125 people. He, his wife Joy, and a good percentage of his core team were greatly impacted by a spiritual outpouring in the first five years of his pastorate. These people have been faithful and God has done great things through True Blue, but M. T. realizes his leadership team is all older men and women. They only have a few youth and young adults. He recognizes the church must reach young people, but he has doubts they would want to come to his church. What would you do if you were M.T.?

LIES ASSOCIATED WITH THIS SCENARIO

- Youth and young adults only cause problems for a ministry.
- I do not have the ability to reach the younger generation.
- We will have to compromise to reach younger people.
- It is not important to find ways to impact the youth.

LIFE AND LEADERSHIP CORE VALUES TO CONSIDER

18   In any people group our ministry wants to influence, I look for the "son of peace" (or "daughter of peace") to work through.
23   I live and demonstrate the gospel supernaturally.
45   I give generously in the areas where I have need.
62   I understand the "times and seasons" of my ministry and what I am supposed to emphasize.
73   I intentionally associate with people who are stronger than me in key areas of life and ministry so I will become stronger in those areas.

DISCERNING WHAT GOD IS DEVELOPING IN ME

- I am learning how to prepare our church for long-lasting influence.
- I have the opportunity to become more relevant.
- I get to help our church get a vision for reaching young people.

QUESTIONS TO ASK BEFORE TAKING ACTION

1. Who are the key young adults we have now to dream with?
2. What have other ministries done about this?
3. What mindsets might be hindering us in this area?
4. Who on our leadership team has the greatest passion for this?
5. What creative ideas do we have?

PRACTICAL STEPS TO CONSIDER

1. **Have a cause worth dying for** – Young people are not prone to come to church because they should, but because they are looking for something to give their lives to. As you preach and live a gospel of commitment to change the world, you will attract the young. Outreaches, missions trips, and participating in causes like sex trafficking will create opportunities for all people (including youth) to have something deep within them touched for Christ and the kingdom.

2. **Create a culture of supernatural encounters** – As your services and ministries grow in the manifest presence of God, you will see young people become transformed and desiring more of what you have. These encounters for them will increase by having regular opportunities for your people to take the love and power of God outside the church walls to the marketplace, the streets, schools, and other places.

3. **Find catalytic young adults to work with and through** – When we want to reach a particular people group, it is vital to find "sons (or daughters) of peace" to primarily invest in (Luke 10:6). Our God is the supplier of all our needs, including important young people to help carry on the calling of the ministry. Once we have identified these catalysts, then we can develop a plan to build our relationships with them (and see what the Lord does).

DECLARATIONS

- Youth and young adults love our church.
- The succession plan in our ministry is setting us up for long-term kingdom advancement.
- Our ministry causes people to have a strong commitment to Jesus and to powerfully impact the world.

ADDITIONAL RESOURCES

VICTORIOUS MINDSETS

What we believe is ultimately more important than what we do. The course of our lives is set by our deepest core beliefs. Our mindsets are either a stronghold for God's purposes or a playhouse for the enemy. In this book, fifty biblical attitudes are revealed that are foundational for those who desire to walk in freedom and power.

CRACKS IN THE FOUNDATION

Going to a higher level in establishing key beliefs will affect ones intimacy with God and fruitfulness for the days ahead. This book challenges many basic assumptions of familiar Bible verses and common Christian phrases that block numerous benefits of our salvation. The truths shared in this book will help fill and repair "cracks" in our thinking which rob us of our God-given potential.

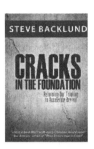

YOU'RE CRAZY IF YOU DON'T TALK TO YOURSELF

Jesus did not just think His way out of the wilderness and neither can we. He spoke truth to invisible beings and mindsets that sought to restrict and defeat Him. This book reveals that life and death are truly in the power of the tongue, and emphasize the necessity of speaking truth to our souls. Our words really do set the course of our lives and the lives of others (Proverbs 18:21, James 3:2-5).

LET'S JUST LAUGH AT THAT

Our hope level is an indicator of whether we are believing truth or lies. Truth creates hope and freedom, but believing lies brings hopelessness and restriction. We can have great theology but still be powerless because of deception about the key issues of life. Many of these self-defeating mindsets exist in our subconscious and have never been identified. This book exposes numerous falsehoods and reveals truth that makes us free. Get ready for a joy-infused adventure into hope-filled living.

ADDITIONAL RESOURCES FROM STEVE AND WENDY BACKLUND

DIVINE STRATEGIES FOR INCREASE

The laws of the spirit are more real than the natural laws. God's laws are primarily principles to release blessing, not rules to be obeyed to gain right standing with God. The Psalmist talks of one whose greatest delight is in the law of the Lord. This delight allows one to discover new aspects of the nature of God (hidden in each law) to behold and worship. The end result of this delighting is a transformed life that prospers in every endeavor. His experience can be our experience, and this book unlocks the blessings hidden in the spiritual realm.

POSSESSING JOY

In His presence is fullness of joy (Psalm 16:11). Joy is to increase as we go deeper in our relationship with God. Religious tradition has devalued the role that gladness and laughter have for personal victory and kingdom advancement. His presence may not always produce joy; but if we never or rarely have fullness of joy, we must reevaluate our concept of God. This book takes one on a journey toward the headwaters of the full joy that Jesus often spoke of. Get ready for joy to increase and strength and longevity to ignite.

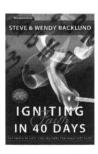

IGNITING FAITH IN 40 DAYS

There must be special seasons in our lives when we break out of routine and do something that will ignite our faith about God and our identity in Christ. This book will lead you through the life-changing experience of a 40-day negativity fast. This fast teaches the power of declaring truth and other transforming daily customs that will strengthen your foundation of faith and radically increase your personal hope.

ADDITIONAL RESOURCES FROM STEVE AND WENDY BACKLUND

ADDITIONAL RESOURCES

LIVING FROM THE UNSEEN

This book will help you identify beliefs that block the reception of God's blessings and hinder our ability to live out our destiny. This book reveals that 1) Believing differently, not trying harder, is the key to change; 2) You cannot do what you don't believe you are; 3) You can only receive what you think you are worth; 4) Rather than learning how to die — it is time to learn how to live.

DECLARATIONS

"Nothing happens in the kingdom unless a declaration is made." Believers everywhere are realizing the power of declarations to empower their lives. You may be wondering, "What are declarations and why are people making them?" or maybe, "Aren't declarations simply a repackaged 'name it and claim' heresy?" Declarations answers these questions by sharing 30 biblical reasons for declaring truth over every area of life. Steve Backlund and his team also answer common objections and concerns to the teaching about declarations. The revelation this book carries will help you to set the direction your life will go. Get ready for 30 days of powerful devotions and declarations that will convince you that life is truly in the power of the tongue.

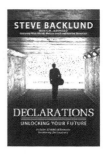

CRUCIAL MOMENTS

This book helps us upgrade how we think, act, and most importantly, believe in those crucial moments when • You feel nervous about speaking in public • Your house is a mess when people come over • A politician whose beliefs oppose yours is elected • You gain more weight than you thought • You don't feel like worshipping and 47 other opportunities for breakthrough.

Audio message series are available through the Igniting Hope store at: IgnitingHope.com.
All books available on Kindle at Amazon.com.

ADDITIONAL RESOURCES FROM STEVE AND WENDY BACKLUND